SSB SIMPLIFIED

A sure-shot formula for clearing the 5-day interview by a former President of the SSB

AIR CMDE NITIN SATHE

Published by
Renu Kaul Verma
Vitasta Publishing Pvt Ltd
4348/4C, Ansari Road, Daryaganj
New Delhi - 110 002
info@vitastapublishing.com

ISBN: 978-81-19670-21-5
© Nitin Sathe
First Edition 2024
MRP ₹295

All Rights Reserved.
No part of this publication may be reproduced, stored in a retrieval system, or transmitted in any form, or by any means–electronic, mechanical, photocopying, recording or otherwise–without the prior permission of the publisher. Opinions expressed in this book are the author's own. The publisher is in no way responsible for these.

Edited by Reena Singh
Layout by Rohit Gautam
Cover Design by Somesh Kumar Mishra
Printed by Vikas Computer and Printers, New Delhi

Contents

Preface	*v*
Who is Eligible to Join the Armed Forces?	*xi*
Introduction	*xiii*
Start Early and Train Best	1
The Written Exam	9
What is Personality?	30
Preparation for the SSB	37
The SWOT Analysis	44
PIQ Form: The Personal Information Questionnaire	50
Day 1 at the SSB: Sifting the Chaff From the Grain	58
The Psychological Test	78
Group Testing	91
A Series of Tests	96

The Interview: One on One	120
The Final Board Interview or Conference	134
Body Language	139
The PABT or CPSS-The Pilot Aptitude Test for IAF Pilot Entry	146

Epilogue *150*

Preface

Why another book on SSB, when there are already so many out there to choose from? Is there something new in this book that should compel you to read it? I assure you there is, for this is new wine in a new bottle!

As a former president of a premier Services Selection Board (SSB), I was able to gain an in-depth understanding of the entire SSB methods and systems. During my tenure, I conducted a comprehensive study of the processes used for selecting future leaders of our armed forces. To further improve the system, I developed a mathematical model of the selection process, identifying what needed enhancement and higher intervention.

The SSB process has been in place for almost 90 years. One can question whether it still suits modern society and whether it addresses the requirements of a new world order. My study revealed that while the system is fundamentally sound, it requires minor adjustments and definitely a change in the assessors' mindset. Some internal changes were implemented during my tenure, and I believe that further improvements have been made in the years since my retirement.

Shedding my uniform after serving for 36 years in the IAF, I got reacquainted with the selection process all over again, this time training young boys and girls at one of the best Armed Forces Preparatory Institutes (AFPIs) in the country.

As SSB president, my role was to administer tests and select the most suitable candidates, without providing feedback or performance debriefs of any kind.

My tenure at AFPI, however, saw a shift in this role. I had to now guide and train candidates on how to successfully navigate the SSB interview process. This required focussing on four key areas:

- Academic preparation for the written exam
- Physical training
- Soft skills development
- SSB-specific training

Our goal was to ensure holistic development that included improving the aspirant's physical and mental endurance, written, and spoken language skills, general awareness, and military knowledge, and all this to be done in just two academic years. With a major chunk of the student's time spent in honing academic skills at school combined with the pressure to do well in their final years, we had only a few months of pure training available for personality development and honing of other skills.

My hands-on experience as Director Training at the National Defence Academy (NDA) came in handy in understanding how young men transform into officers with military bearing over four years. Long ago, I had been an NDA cadet, myself, and later its training head. This, along with my roles at SSB and AFPI, I believe have given me a 360-degree perspective on grooming candidates for the armed forces.

It was my students who encouraged me to write this book in an easy-to-understand story format, combining my knowledge and experience. This book is unique in that it provides specific guidance without promoting shortcuts to success that training institutes seem to be doing. The insights here are applicable not only to NDA aspirants but to all candidates seeking entry into the armed forces through any of its entry schemes.

I leave you with ten golden tips for success at cracking the written exam which one has to pass to graduate onto the SSB interview. You will also find these tips amplified throughout this book. Revisit these tips as frequently as possible to maintain the right focus and tempo for your exams.

Ten tips for success in the written exam

1. **Have confidence in yourself and your preparation.** When you get stressed at the thought of the exam and are unsure of some aspects of your studies, do not panic. Close your eyes and say 'relax, relax, relax' in your mind while clenching and unclenching your fists. This will surely make you relax. I have tried it myself, and it works! The exam will have questions from areas and subjects that you have studied for this long and you should not be unduly worried.
2. **Be consistent with your preparations.** Remember to continue to study till a day before the exam after which you should just go through the various formulae and concentrate on the short tricks of answering questions

that you have been taught. Don't cram on the last day, because it will only lead to confusion! Practice, practice and only practice helps, especially in the mathematics paper. Attempt as many mock tests as you can.
3. **Learn the art of relaxation between bouts of study.** Do not keep staring at your books and notes when you are mentally tired. Take a break and start afresh for better assimilation.
4. **Ensure that you travel to your centre, a day before your exam.** Unwind after your journey, sleep well, and wake up fresh for the gruelling tests. Avoid caffeine as far as possible.
5. **Be well prepared with the stationery.** Remember, smart watches, phones and electronic gadgets are not permitted at the centre. Carry an energy bar and something to eat between the two papers. Carry water and, of course, your mask, if needed!
6. **As you are seated for the exam waiting for the question paper, close your eyes and meditate.** Tell yourself to relax. Say to yourself that you are well prepared and that you are going to do your best. The heart will beat a little fast and you will be stressed, but any exercise such as telling yourself to relax and clenching and unclenching your fists to reduce anxiety helps. Remember, those around you are in the same predicament!
7. **Maxing the math paper.** You will be running against time for this. Attempt the sections you are most confident about, at first. When you initially read through the paper, write the formula to be used for certain questions so that you don't waste time thinking later. If the paper is hard or moderately hard, aim to get 50 to 60 correct answers to make it to the cut off in this paper; anything more is

bonus! Remember, the better you score, the better merit you get! Do not get flustered if you cannot answer a question; just go to the next one and return to this one later. And yes, most importantly, check and recheck if you are marking the answer on the Optical Mark Recognition (OMR) sheet correctly!

8. **The GAT paper is the easier one and you will be more relaxed for this.** Do not worry about what happened in the earlier paper as you answer this paper. Attempt the English section first, followed by General Science and General Knowledge sections. Skip to the next question if you are not sure of an answer and revisit this later after completing the paper.

9. **DO NOT attempt to answer by fluke.** Remember, there are negative marks for wrong answers. I have known several aspirants who have spoilt their chance by taking chances!

10. **Wishing you all success and may you crack the written exam with high marks!** After you pass, we shall prepare for the Services Selection Board interview.

★ ★ ★

All the best and do well!

Who is Eligible to Join the Armed Forces?

The eligibility criteria for the various entry schemes to join the armed forces is listed here.

Male and female unmarried candidates who fit the age criteria (16.5 to 19.5 years on the day of joining) are permitted to attempt the NDA written exam which is conducted twice a year in April and September. The qualifying requirements are given at the NDA website, nda.nic.in as well as the UPSC site.

For joining the army, candidates who are pursuing any stream in the 11th and 12th class are allowed to appear. However, for the Indian Air Force and the Indian Navy, science stream with Physics, Chemistry and Mathematics is mandatory for aspiring candidates.

It must be noted here that the UPSC written exam remains the same for all candidates where the thrust is on Mathematics as well as the sciences, and therefore, candidates who are pursuing science stream would be at an advantage. Army aspirants who do not have science and mathematics would have to put in extra effort to attain proficiency in these subjects.

I would recommend that NDA aspirants opt for the science stream (PCM), irrespective of the service they want to choose. They then will also have the flexibility to apply for a change of service during their training at the NDA.

For selection criteria to join the armed forces through the Combined Defence Services (CDS) exam, the eligibility criteria are given at (upsc.gov.in).

For selection criteria to join the Army through the Technical Entry Scheme, you may like to visit (joinindianarmy.nic.in).

For selection criteria to join the Indian Navy, you can visit Selection procedure - Join Indian Navy | Government of India

For selection criteria to join the IAF through the Air Force Central Admission Test (AFCAT) entry, you are advised to visit (cdac.in).

There are a plethora of websites on which criteria are specified but the ones I have listed here are government websites where you will get the correct, updated information. The criteria are subject to change and you must look for the latest information available on the above websites when you decide to apply.

When you finally clear the exams and are called for the interview, you have to emerge a winner at the five-day series of tests at the SSB.

Introduction

> The beautiful thing about learning is that nobody can take it away from you.
>
> —B B King

As the President of the Services Selection Board, I had seen thousands of candidates going through the most gruelling of interviews just like the way I had done many, many years ago. Later, as president of the Board, I had assessed many of them for their personality traits. It was a learning experience of a lifetime.

As president and head of the SSB, I was able to understand the detailed nuances of testing as well as incorporate many positive changes in the system. I also saw thousands of aspirants lining up week after week at the gates with hope in their eyes, praying to the Almighty to help them join the armed forces and, thereby, be a part of all the good things associated with it.

I was not happy though, to see some good boys and girls go back disappointed, when I knew for certain that they had it in them to be part of the Indian Defence Forces. At that point, I couldn't help them, but I knew for certain that one day, I would write a simple-to-understand and executable mantra in the form of a small book to help such aspirants make it to the finish line.

Unfortunately, one is not allowed to 'debrief' candidates on their performance or tell them what went wrong. Therefore, quite literally, the SSB learning was rather one-sided for me.

I am aware that there are a lot of books available on the subject and even more are in the offing. I, however, plan to take you through the process of testing in my own, different way. It is not for me to give you shortcuts to success, nor to give you the 'inside' story of the SSB of how things work behind the scenes (that would be going against morals and principles), but to give you certain directions and guidance, which if followed in letter and spirit, can help you achieve your dream.

No classes of instructions and training can 'teach' a candidate how to crack the Services Selection Board interview. The tests you can be mentally prepared for, but you must also know what is going to confront you in the five days of the interview process. Other than that, this book will take you through some simple steps to help you improve your personality profile. These are more to do with practice and a change in thinking and attitude.

My advice is that you start preparations as soon as you decide to join this profession. It is not like other exams for which you need to prepare according to the syllabus and forget about what you learnt once the test is over.

And once you have cleared your exams, you will be called for the five-day interview process at the SSB and finally, when it is time for the results to be declared, the candidate is only told whether he or she made the grade or not. Disappointed candidates go back home and try to analyse what went wrong. This self-analysis is, more often than not, incorrect. I can say this with certainty.

The technique of testing and the process may seem simple

to an outsider, but it is among the most scientifically designed series of tests that you are made to go through. It will, therefore, be incorrect for anyone who does not make it, to pass judgement about what went wrong or point fingers at a system which has proved itself, over and over again, and over so many years.

The answer lies in preparing well after understanding what will come in the series of tests in those five days. One just needs to organise well for these. By preparing well, I do not mean that you mug up answers, write politically, morally, and socially correct answers, or learn shortcuts to success.

Your preparation starts as soon as you decide to join the armed forces. Remember, it is who you actually are that matters and not what you project.

The name of the game, therefore, is to improve yourself in all spheres.

Naturally, you will ask what one can do to improve oneself. For starters, go through this book meticulously.

Besides the many things that will be discussed, start by understanding yourself. Do a Strength-Weakness-Opportunities-Threat (SWOT) analysis and write down all that you feel are your positives, negatives and what are the obstacles that prevent you from achieving what you want. Once you do that, you would have projected your real self on paper. This 'self-mapping' will make you 'see' what or who you are. You do not have to tell the results of this analysis to anyone! This will automatically show you the path or paths to maximise your strengths and to improve your weaknesses.

Begin by asking yourself why you should join the armed forces. Look around and check out the jobs available in the market. There are so many of them, but, only a *few* are as exciting as a job in uniform.

There could be a thousand reasons why you want to join the armed forces. A few important ones are listed below and you could list out more which relate to you as you carry out your self-introspection.

- A job in the armed forces is not a job but a way of life. Every day is a new day at work and takes you through novel and varied challenges which makes your job even more interesting.
- You make the best of friends in the armed forces.
- You get genuine respect for what you do.
- You get many perks and privileges for you and your family.
- Your improved quality of life ensures that you remain healthy, wealthy, and wise; at the same time, you get enough time to pursue your interests and passions.
- The armed forces gives you a life of quality which is passed down to your young ones and future generations, too.

So, are you in or out? Since you have made an effort to buy this book, I figure you are really interested and rearing to go. Do not miss out on a great life, a life lived with honour, and a life lived to the fullest. Work hard now to get in.

Start Early and Train Best

> Leadership and learning are indispensable to each other.
> –John F Kennedy

If someone asks me when is the right time to start working towards joining our armed forces, I would answer, 'Yesterday!' It is always good to start early and prepare well. That is always sound advice. What, with all this competition, you need to be the best among the best! So, once you have decided the path that you want to take, start preparations for countering the good, bad and the ugly that you are inevitably going to encounter.

Well begun, is half done—just remember this!

As you read through this book, you will realise that there is not much that you need to do. It is just the basic simple path to becoming a good all-rounder, a person who has knowledge (power of the mind), physical and mental courage, social skills and confidence in your abilities. In short, you must develop all that it takes to be a good human being and a model citizen!

If I were to join the armed forces again, I would, for a start, take the following steps besides the self-analysis or understanding that I spoke about. We shall be discussing these in detail as we go along.

1. **Medical fitness and exercise:** Start exercising regularly if you don't do so already, to remain medically fit. It would be a good idea to get examined at a hospital to see if you fit into the medical standards as prescribed. While there may be treatment(s) available to get rid of some irregularities, there may be some kinks in your body which may make you permanently unfit for armed forces life. Ascertain that all is well, then move on with the preparations.

   For example, I am often asked by candidates that they have an eyesight issue and would like to undergo Lasix surgery. This surgery may improve your eyesight to the desired standards, but it is not permitted for younger age groups wanting to join NDA. Some aspirants say they have colour blindness and I advise them to go to the doctor to see if their level of colour blindness is acceptable or not. Colour blindness in any degree is not permitted in the Air Force and the Navy.

   In addition, take up team games like football, hockey, volleyball and basketball; these games help you in more ways than just fitness.

2. **Start reading:** Reading is beneficial for you, whether it is fiction, non-fiction, comics, newspapers, or magazines. Reading improves your language skills and articulation, besides making you aware of what is happening around you. This is an important aspect, and is checked at many phases of the SSB process. Reading provides exercise to the brain, improves concentration, increases general

knowledge, is motivational, and reduces stress.

In addition, a good idea would be to read a General Knowledge book like the *Competition Success Review* or something similar.

3. **Start writing:** Read an article or book and write a small paragraph on what you learnt from it in your own words. Look at a picture or a scene for a few seconds and write a short story on what it makes you feel about what is happening and what could the situation depicted in the picture lead to. Writing improves memory function and language skills and helps you to be coherent. Good articulation helps you in many ways at the SSB.

   To improve your vocabulary, get a dictionary or check out an online one. Every day, attempt to know five to six new and random words. Try and use them in your everyday writing and conversations. But first, write and understand their meanings. Do it multiple times till you are comfortable with these new words.

   Remember, to be a decent writer and speaker, a vocabulary of about 8,000 words is good enough. You could improve your vocabulary in any other way you deem fit.

4. **Develop a sense of curiosity:** This is a laudable trait. Be curious about everything and develop an inquisitive nature. You need to learn to apply your academic knowledge into practical aspects of life. Look at the things around you that help you with your daily life such as the fan, fridge, pressure cooker, cycle, car, watch and things like that. How do they work? What is the principle of their operation and the science behind these little gadgets

that make your life comfortable? Ask the **How, Why, Where** and **What** of their working. Keep a note of all these gadgets that you study about in a diary and know the concepts behind their working. This exercise will make you wiser and more aware of your surroundings and bring about a marked change in your confidence levels.

5. **Make lots of friends:** Friendships are an important part of personality development. You get to understand human relationships, understand that each person is different and behaves differently to the same inputs. Interacting with others also makes you socially acceptable.

   All work in the armed forces is team work and one deals with humans all the time, whether at work, play and even in war.

6. **Know your armed forces**: When you want to go for a movie, you like to do some research on it to see if it is worth the effort. Similarly, you research a product online before you buy it.

   On similar lines, it would be a good idea to get to know some basic information about where you are headed and which service you would like to join! In your interview, you would be expected to know a little of the services in general and about your choice of service in particular.

   For example, an Air Force aspirant should know about the aircrafts in the IAF, the physics of flying, the regional commands of the IAF, how many men and officers serve there, and know about training aircraft and things like that. If you are to join the NDA, IMA, OTA or AFA, find out a little about these institutions. A lot of information is available on the internet on all the training institutions, their daily routine and their organisational structure.

Keep jotting down all you have learnt in a diary or notebook. I like to call this a 'Gen-Book.' Make one immediately. All knowledge, including knowledge of our armed forces will always be beneficial in the long run.

7. **Pick up a hobby**: Developing interest in extra co-curricular activities further shapes your personality. Most hobbies qualify as extracurricular activities when you practice them in an organised way as part of a club or team. These develop new skills, shape your mental health, and improve social connections. They also help you in application of what you have learnt in the classroom—your academic skills in real world concepts, and is an important part of a well-rounded education.

    Try and join an NGO or an organisation committed to helping the world be a better place. In my years as an assessor, I found that many candidates write about being part of an NGO, but when quizzed about it, they are not able to say much! My advice, therefore, would be to join such ventures only if you are really interested and not just to impress or to put it on your resume!

8. **Study harder:** This is key. You must put in more effort than usual to crack the written exam to obtain good marks. Check out the syllabus for each exam. The syllabus will surely have something additional to what is taught at school or college. You will need additional books or go back to your teacher for supplementary coaching. That apart, you need to know the basics of each subject that have

been taught and understand the concepts well. I would recommend that you read up on your maths, science, and social studies books of class 6 onwards. You may think that you know it all there, but just try and go through these text books once again and see how it helps you to refresh your memory. A good foundation of knowledge and depth of understanding will stand you in good stead as you prepare for the exams and the SSB.

That is all for starters. As we continue discussing the details of the SSB in this book, we will know some specific areas for development applicable to the specific tests that are described in detail. The five days of the selection process are highly educative and are an experience you will never forget, even if you do not make it to the armed forces.

To this day, I remember the tests that I went through at my SSB vividly. I made lifelong friends during the five days of staying together and this stood me in good stead in many aspects of life as a soldier as well as a human being.

By preparing in the correct manner, you will improve your chances of making it through merit. For this, you need to get serious. But that doesn't mean that you should approach one of the many 'money earning' institutes who, to say the least, are often mechanical in their approach and only tell you shortcuts to success. I am convinced that these shortcuts do not work at all.

The SSB assessors are looking for the 'real' you and not the 'projected' you. So, the way you sit, fold your hands, walk, speak, and carry yourself as taught in these short courses will not help you at all. At the SSB, assessors can make out immediately if you have been trained incorrectly—and that would be a wrong starting point for any aspirant.

Does one benefit by reading about SSB on the internet? Well, yes and no. I would, rather dissuade you from preparing for the SSB from websites. Understand in letter and spirit, what I am trying to convey here.

The internet gives out a whole lot of unnecessary information about the SSB, and has many people giving out personal but fictitious stories about things that happen at the selection centre. I can say with conviction that most of this information is like a WhatsApp forward, mostly false and fake that some of us are in the habit of forwarding without ascertaining its authenticity.

While browsing through the internet, I came across a video of a boy who said he had cleared his SSB in some sixth or seventh attempt. He spoke about how a cup of tea was offered to him during the interview and how the interviewing officer even offered him a cigarette! It was an absolutely absurd and concocted story!

So, avoid learning about SSB from the internet. Perhaps, you could familiarise yourself with the process from there, but ensure that you clarify your doubts from an expert only. Just like an overload of information on how to go about doing a new task leaves you muddled, similarly, the many internet sites that you may visit could leave you confused and not much wiser.

The internet will also give out concepts and the inner secrets behind solving the tests and how evaluation is done, what are the qualities that you are being assessed for and how candidates can hide certain facts about themselves. That, I assure you, is not an aspect you need to know. It would be best to not venture into that area. After all, we must leave some things for the assessors to do, don't you agree?

For those of you who have already gone into the science behind the tests, about how many qualities you are judged on, what personality attributes mean etc., then, I would advise you to delete all that from your memory. This kind of superfluous information interferes with your performance while you attempt the tests at the SSB. Avoid this and do not fall prey to falsified information perpetrated on the internet.

To summarise, while it is good to be aware of what tests are going to be conducted, it is totally incorrect and undesirable to know what happens behind the scenes. Let the assessors, who are experts at their jobs, do their bit while you do yours.

So, let's first get on with the preparation for the written exams.

The Written Exam

It is a miracle that curiosity survives formal education.
–Albert Einstein

Now that you have decided to attempt and have the determination to be a part of our armed forces, let us delve into the preparation for the written exam. It goes without saying that the more marks you obtain in your written exam, more the chances of making it into the merit list, once you clear the SSB.

I have often found candidates aiming for the lowest mark or 'cut-off,' and then not making it into the merit list because of this. So, now that you have the time, get into study mode, and give it your best shot! Do not think of attempting a trial at first and then making a serious second attempt. Let the first one be the best and the final one, and I am sure that you will make the grade if you follow the guidelines given in this book.

The following table gives out the various entry schemes and the exams associated with them.

The maximum number of candidates who join our armed forces are through four major entry schemes, **NDA, CDS, AFCAT/INET** and **TES**. The rest of the schemes have very few vacancies and are specialist entries.

S.NO	TYPE OF ENTRY	NAME OF EXAM	EXAMINATION SCHEDULE	REMARKS
1.	NDA & NA	UPSC NDA Written	Twice a year	Cut off marks not constant
2.	IMA-DIRECT ENTRY	UPSC CDS Exam	Twice a year	Cut off marks not constant
3.	AFCAT/INET	AFCAT (BY IAF), INET by NAVY	Twice a year	Cut off marks not constant
4.	TES (10+2)	Applicable for army entry		NO EXAM, Cut off marks are as per your rank in JEE and your 12th class.
5.	TGC			No exam
6.	SSC (TECH)			No exam
7.	NCC SPECIAL ENTRY			'C' certificate No exam
8.	JAG ENTRY			Vacancy based
9.	SSC (WOMEN)			Same as men SSC
10.	ACC ENTRY			No exam
11.	SCO SCHEME			JCO/NCO 28-35 yrs age
	PC (SL)			JCO/or upto 42 yrs age/10 yrs service, SSC pass

Note: Please find out the latest available entry schemes from the official websites; these are subject to change.

Once you have passed the requisite exam for a particular entry scheme, you will receive a call letter for your testing at the Services Selection Board. The testing is the same for each class of entrant, and therefore, there is no separate testing methodology. One is not required to prepare differently for these.

What is different, however, is the syllabus for the exam for each type of entry. Let us go through each of the syllabi for the written tests. Please reconfirm these from the official website since changes are incorporated from time to time.

Broadly speaking, the 'non-UPSC' exams are a bit easier than the UPSC exams. The following paragraphs list out the subjects that have to be studied. The papers are strictly set as per the weightage of the contents of the subjects and therefore, you will know which areas you need to stress upon.

National Defence Academy
NDA - Maths (300 Marks)

The basic subjects are listed in the table below:

• Algebra	• Matrices Determinants	• Trigonometry
• Differential Calculus	• Analytical Geometry 2D & 3D	• Integral Calculus
• Differential Equations	• Vector Algebra	• Probability

Details of topics under each of the above are given below:

1. **Algebra**
   Concept of set, operations on sets, Venn diagrams, De Morgan laws, Cartesian product, relation, equivalence relation, Representation of real numbers on a line, Complex numbers—basic properties, modulus, argument, cube roots of unity, Binary system of numbers, Conversion of a number in decimal system to binary system and vice-versa, Arithmetic, Geometric and Harmonic progressions, Quadratic equations with real coefficients, Solution of linear inequations of two variables by graphs, Permutation and Combination, Binomial theorem and its applications, Logarithms and their applications.

2. **Matrices and Determinants**
   Types of matrices, operations on matrices, Determinant of a matrix, basic properties of determinants, Adjoint and inverse of a square matrix, Applications—Solution of a system of linear equations in two or three unknowns by Cramer's rule and by Matrix Method.

3. **Trigonometry**
   Angles and their measures in degrees and in radians, Trigonometrical ratios, Trigonometric identities, Sum and difference formulae, Multiple and Sub-multiple angles, Inverse trigonometric functions, Applications—Height and distance, properties of triangles.

4. **Differential Calculus**
   Concept of a real valued function—domain, range and graph of a function. Composite functions, one to one, onto and inverse functions. Notion of limit, Standard

limits—examples. Continuity of functions—examples, algebraic operations on continuous functions. Derivative of function at a point, geometrical and physical interpretation of a derivative—applications. Derivatives of sum, product and quotient of functions, derivative of a function with respect to another function, derivative of a composite function. Second order derivatives. Increasing and decreasing functions. Application of derivatives in problems of maxima and minima.

5. **Analytical Geometry of Two & Three Dimensions**
   Rectangular Cartesian Coordinate system, Distance formula, Equation of a line in various forms, Angle between two lines, Distance of a point from a line, Equation of a circle in standard and in general form, Standard forms of parabola, ellipse, and hyperbola. Eccentricity and axis of a conic, Point in a three-dimensional space, distance between two points, Direction Cosines and direction ratios, Equation two points, Equation of a plane and a line in various forms, Angle between two lines and angle between two planes, Equation of a sphere.

6. **Integral Calculus and Differential Equations**
   Integration as inverse of differentiation, integration by substitution and by parts, standard integrals involving algebraic expressions, trigonometric, exponential, and hyperbolic functions. Evaluation of definite integrals—determination of areas of plane regions bounded by curves—applications. Definition of order and degree of a differential equation, formation of a differential equation by examples. General and particular solutions

of differential equations, solution of first order and first-degree differential equations of various types—examples. Application in problems of growth and decay.

7. **Vector Algebra**
Vectors in two and three dimensions, magnitude and direction of a vector. Unit and null vectors, addition of vectors, scalar multiplication of a vector, scalar product, or dot product of two vectors. Vector product or cross product of two vectors. Applications—work done by a force and moment of a force and in geometrical problems.

8. **Statistics and Probability**
Statistics: Classification of data, Frequency distribution, cumulative frequency distribution—examples. Graphical representation—Histogram, Pie Chart, frequency polygon—examples. Measures of Central tendency—Mean, median and mode. Variance and standard deviation—determination and comparison. Correlation and regression. Probability: Random experiment, outcomes and associated sample space, events, mutually exclusive and exhaustive events, impossible and certain events. Union and Intersection of events. Complementary, elementary, and composite events. Definition of probability—classical and statistical—examples. Elementary theorems on probability—simple problems. Conditional probability, Bayes' theorem—simple problems. Random variable as function on a sample space. Binomial distribution, examples of random experiments giving rise to Binomial distribution.

General Knowledge (Maximum Marks: 400)

This test will consist of six sections. Candidates will have to prepare the basics of all these sections given below:

Physics	Chemistry	General Science
History	Geography	Current Affairs

The question paper on General Knowledge will broadly cover the above subjects under the following sub-topics.

Section 'A' (Physics)

Physical Properties and States of Matter, Mass, Weight, Volume, Density and Specific Gravity, Principle of Archimedes, Pressure Barometer. Motion of objects, Velocity and Acceleration, Newton's Laws of Motion, Force and Momentum, Parallelogram of Forces, Stability and Equilibrium of bodies, Gravitation, Elementary ideas of work, Power, and Energy. Effects of Heat, Measurement of Temperature and Heat, Change of State and Latent Heat, Modes of transference of Heat. Sound waves and their properties, Simple musical instruments. Rectilinear Propagation of Light, Reflection, and refraction. Spherical mirrors and Lenses, Human Eye. Natural and Artificial Magnets, Properties of a Magnet, Earth as a Magnet, Static and Current Electricity, Conductors and Non-conductors, Ohm's Law, Simple Electrical Circuits, Heating, Lighting and Magnetic effects of Current, Measurement of Electrical Power, Primary and Secondary Cells, Use of X-Rays. General Principles in the working of the following: Simple Pendulum, Simple Pulleys, Siphon, Levers, Balloon, Pumps, Hydrometer, Pressure Cooker, Thermos Flask, Gramophone,

Telegraphs, Telephone, Periscope, Telescope, Microscope, Mariner's Compass; Lightening Conductors, Safety Fuses.

Section 'B' (Chemistry)

Physical and Chemical changes. Elements, Mixtures and Compounds, Symbols, Formulae and simple Chemical Equations, Law of Chemical Combination (excluding problems). Properties of Air and Water. Preparation and Properties of Hydrogen, Oxygen, Nitrogen and Carbon dioxide, Oxidation and Reduction. Acids, bases, and salts. Carbon—different forms. Fertilizers—Natural and Artificial. Material used in the preparation of substances like Soap, Glass, Ink, Paper, Cement, Paints, Safety Matches and Gun-Powder. Elementary ideas about the structure of Atoms, Atomic Equivalent and Molecular Weights, Valency.

Section 'C' (General Science)

Difference between living and non-living. Basis of Life—Cells, Protoplasm and Tissues. Growth and Reproduction in Plants and Animals. Elementary knowledge of Human Body and its important organs. Common Epidemics, their causes and prevention. Food—Source of Energy for man. Constituents of food, Balanced Diet. The Solar System—Meteors and Comets, Eclipses. Achievements of Eminent Scientists.

Section 'D'
(History, Freedom Movement etc.)

A broad survey of Indian History, with emphasis on Culture and Civilisation. Freedom Movement in India. Elementary study of Indian Constitution and Administration. Elementary knowledge of Five-Year Plans of India. NITI Aayog, Panchayati

Raj, Co-operatives and Community Development. Bhoodan, Sarvodaya, National Integration and Welfare State, Basic Teachings of Mahatma Gandhi. Forces shaping the modern world; Renaissance, Exploration and Discovery; War of American Independence. French Revolution, Industrial Revolution and Russian Revolution. Impact of Science and Technology on Society. Concept of one World, United Nations, Panchsheel, Democracy, Socialism and Communism. Role of India in the present world.

Section 'E' (Geography)
The Earth, its shape and size. Latitudes and Longitudes, Concept of time. International Date Line. Movements of Earth and their effects. Origin of Earth. Rocks and their classification; Weathering—Mechanical and Chemical, Earthquakes and Volcanoes. Ocean Currents and Tides Atmosphere and its composition; Temperature and Atmospheric Pressure, Planetary Winds, Cyclones and Anti-cyclones; Humidity; Condensation and Precipitation; Types of Climate, Major Natural regions of the World. Regional Geography of India—Climate, Natural vegetation. Mineral and Power resources; location and distribution of agricultural and Industrial activities. Important Sea ports and main sea, land and air routes of India. Main items of Imports and Exports of India.

Section 'F' (Current Events)
Knowledge of Important events that have happened in India in the recent years. Current important world events. Prominent personalities—both Indian and International including those connected with cultural activities and sports.

English Syllabus: NDA
- Grammar and usage
- Comprehension and cohesion
- Spotting of errors
- Paragraph jumbling
- Fill in the blanks
- Synonyms and antonyms
- Vocabulary
- Cloze test
- Sentence correction and improvement
- Idioms and proverbs
- Completion of sentence

2. Combined Defence Services (CDS) Exam

Math Syllabus

Number System
Natural numbers, Integers, Rational and Real numbers. Fundamental operations, addition, subtraction, multiplication, division, Square roots, Decimal fractions. Unitary method, time and distance, time and work, percentages, applications to simple and compound interest, profit and loss, ratio and proportion, variation.
Elementary Number Theory
Division algorithm. Prime and composite numbers. Tests of divisibility by 2, 3, 4, 5, 9 and 11. Multiples and factors. Factorisation Theorem. H.C.F. and L.C.M. Euclidean algorithm. Logarithms to base 10, laws of logarithms, use of logarithmic tables.

Algebra

Basic Operations, simple factors, Remainder Theorem, H.C.F., L.C.M., Theory of polynomials, solutions of quadratic equations, relation between its roots and coefficients (Only real roots to be considered). Simultaneous linear equations in two unknowns—analytical and graphical solutions. Simultaneous linear inequations in two variables and their solutions. Practical problems leading to two simultaneous linear equations or inequations in two variables or quadratic equations in one variable & their solutions. Set language and set notation, Rational expressions and conditional identities, Laws of indices.

Trigonometry

Sine ×, cosine ×, Tangent × when $0° < × < 90°$ Values of sin ×, cos × and tan ×, for ×= $0°, 30°, 45°, 60°$ and $90°$ Simple trigonometric identities. Use of trigonometric tables. Simple cases of heights and distances.

Geometry

Lines and angles, Plane and plane figures, Theorems on (i) Properties of angles at a point, (ii) Parallel lines, (iii) Sides and angles of a triangle, (iv) Congruency of triangles, (v) Similar triangles, (vi) Concurrence of medians and altitudes, (vii) Properties of angles, sides and diagonals of a Parallelogram, rectangle and square, (viii) Circles and its properties including tangents and normals, (ix) Loci.

Mensuration

Areas of squares, rectangles, parallelograms, triangle and circle. Areas of figures which can be split up into these figures (Field Book), Surface area and volume of cuboids, lateral surface and volume of right circular cones and cylinders, surface area and volume of spheres.

> **Statistics**
> Collection and tabulation of statistical data, Graphical representation frequency polygons, histograms, bar charts, pie charts etc. Measures of central tendency.

English Syllabus
- Spotting errors questions
- Sentence arrangement questions
- Synonyms and antonyms
- Selecting words
- Ordering of Sentence
- Comprehension questions
- Ordering of words in a sentence
- Fill in the blanks questions
- Idioms and phrases

General Knowledge Syllabus
- Economics
- Physics
- Current Affairs
- Politics
- Chemistry
- Sociology
- History
- Defence-related Awards
- Geography
- Environment
- Sports
- Biology
- Cultural

3. Air Force Central Admission Test (AFCAT)

General Awareness	History, Geography, Civics, Politics, Current Affairs, Environment basic science, Defence, Art culture, Sports etc.
English	Comprehension, Error Detection, Sentence Completion/Filling in of the correct word, Synonyms, Antonyms, and Testing of word, Vocabulary, Idioms and Phrases
Numerical Ability	Decimal Fraction, Time and Work, Average, Profit and Loss, Percentage, Ratio and Proportion and Simple Interest, Time and Distance (trains/boats and streams)
Reasoning and military aptitude test	Verbal Skill and Spatial Ability

Indian Navy Entrance Test

The Indian Navy Entrance Test has four sections with their subjects as mentioned below:

Section 1
English (25 Marks)

Comprehension, Usage of Words, Sentence completion/ Corrections, Punctuation, Grammar, Vocabulary, Antonyms and Synonyms, Parts of Speech, Direct and Indirect Speech, Idioms and Phrases, Active and Passive Voice etc. (Question paper will be designed to test the candidates' understanding of English and working use of Grammar.)

Section 2
Reasoning and Numerical Ability (25 Marks)

Spatial, Numerical, Reasoning and Associative Ability,

Sequences, Spellings, Unscrambling, Coding and Decoding, Missing Numbers/Series Completion, Decimal Fraction, Ratios and Proportion, Average and Volume, Time and Work, Speed and Distance, Market Price, Cash Price, Expenditure Problems, Profit and Loss, Percentage, Factoring (LCM and HCF), Simple Interest and Compound Interest, Mensuration Formulas (Calculation of length, breadth or height of square, rectangle, cube etc.)

Section 3
General Science & Mathematical Aptitude (25 Marks)
Nature of Matter, Universe, Electricity and its Applications, Force and Gravitation, Newton's Laws of Motion, Work, Energy and Power, Heat, Temperature, Light, Current, Magnetism, Metals and Non Metals, Measurements, Sound and Wave Motion, Atomic Structure, Chemistry—Carbon and its Compounds, Periodic Table, Acids, Bases & Salts, Food, Nutrition and Health Physiology and Human Diseases and Basic Computer Science Arithmetic Ability, Number Systems, Algebra, Basic Trigonometry, Geometry, Statistics, Probability and Set Theory.

Section 4
General Knowledge (25 Marks)
History of India, Geography, Climate/Environment, Civics—Constitution of India, Art, Culture, Dance, Heritage, Religion, Freedom Movement, Important National Facts, Economics, Politics, Sports and Championships, Entertainment, Books and Authors, Awards, Defence and Wars, Geographical Neighbours, Countries—Languages, Capitals, Currencies, Common Name, Full Forms, Abbreviations, Eminent Personalities, National—

Bird/Animal/Monuments/Flower/Anthem/Sport/Flag/Emblem etc, Discoveries and Current Affairs.

The table below gives you the approximate number of hours of study an average student should put in for each subject. You know best what subjects you are good at; and therefore, you can increase or decrease the amount of effort required for yourself. This rough calculation is based on the weightage of each subject and the proficiency required in each, and the minimum number of hours of study that you will have to carry out to crack the exam.

		NDA		
S.No	TYPE OF ENTRY	SUBJECT	TOTAL HOURS	REMARKS
1	NDA/NAVAC	Math	180	Thrust on maths
		Physics	40	
		Chemistry	25	
		Biology	25	
		General knowledge	75	
		English	50	
	TOTAL		395	

CDS

S.No	TYPE OF ENTRY	SUBJECT	TOTAL HOURS	REMARKS
1	IMA/OTA/AFA/NAVAC	Math	80	Thrust on Math and GK
		Physics	40	
		Chemistry	25	
		Biology	18	
		General knowledge	110	
		English	45	
	TOTAL		318	

AFCAT/INCAT

S.No	TYPE OF ENTRY	SUBJECT	TOTAL HOURS	REMARKS
1	AFA/NAVAC	Math + reasoning	75	
		English	30	
		General knowledge	45	
	TOTAL		150	

From the syllabi above, it is amply clear that you need to get your mathematics up to speed and need to give maximum attention to this subject. This may require you to go back to the basics taught in class eighth, ninth and tenth. You may also have to go into subjects that are not in your board syllabus. I recommend that you go to a tutor or join the classes for IIT/JEE. On the same lines, this applies to other subjects in the syllabus where you may need to get your concepts clear.

Plan your studies in such a manner that you complete the entire syllabus at least one month in advance of the exam. Keep the last month for mock tests and revisions. Mock test series are available in books as well as on the net. Take these tests with all sincerity and see that you become proficient in answering the questions in the time allotted.

The tests are always a race against time, and the candidate who is better prepared and has his basics right, ends up doing well. The questions have negative marking; therefore, be very careful when you choose the questions that you are going to attempt. We shall discuss more about this when we talk about what happens at the examination centre.

It is time now to make a realistic timetable, and stick to it as far as possible, giving yourself some spare days to cater for exigencies. If you start well in time, then you will be able to have a happy mix of studies, play and entertainment too. We always tend to blame the paucity of time when we ourselves begin late!

The 10 tips to success I had mentioned in the preface to the book will come in useful during your preparatory phase. Here they are again:
- **Have confidence in yourself and your preparation.** If stressed, close your eyes and tell yourself to 'relax.'

- **Be consistent.** Only practice helps, especially in the mathematics paper.
- **Learn the art of relaxation between bouts of study.** Ensure that you take regular breaks.
- **Reach your centre, a day before the exams.** Unwind after your journey, sleep well, and wake up fresh for the tests.
- **Be well prepared with stationery and don't carry electronic gadgets.** Keep an energy bar to nibble on between the two papers.
- **While waiting for the question paper, close your eyes and meditate.** And tell yourself to relax.
- **Max the math paper.** Even if math is not your subject, follow a strategy to see yourself through. Attempt the questions you know and aim to make the cutoff in this paper.
- **Relax for the easier GAT paper.** Attempt the English section first, followed by General Science and General Knowledge sections.
- **Don't answer by fluke.** There are negative marks for wrong answers, so don't do guesswork.
- **Crack the written exam!** After you pass, it's time to prepare for the Services Selection Board interview.

The exam

Finally, the date of the exam will draw near and your nerves may show signs of fraying. For the last few days, just go through important formulae, theorems, shortcuts to solving problems, and memorise some of the data that is important. Meditate to keep your mind calm and alert.

Get ready with the physical requirements of the exam. Make sure you have your exam entry papers, identity card, writing material etc. Ensure that you have gone through the instructions about the conduct of the exam thoroughly. Do not miss out on any point, however trivial, which may cause you trouble and mental agony just before the test, thereby leading to poor performance.

I remember boys forgetting their identity cards in their cars and then panicking when they were not allowed to go out of the centre or to use their mobile phone to retrieve the situation.

It would be a good idea to relax and recuperate one day prior to the exam. You have put in a gruelling few months of hard work, and your mind needs rest before the exam. Eat wisely and avoid caffeine. Get a good night's sleep before the exam day.

Arrive at the centre well in time and look for the room allotted to you. Leave all your troubles and problems outside the class along with your bag and notes. Enter the exam hall in a happy state of mind, carrying all the required things with you.

The heart would be all aflutter as you settle down into your seat. Just know that you have prepared well and tell yourself that you are going to do well. After all, they are not going to give you any question out of the syllabus, neither are you being checked for your knowledge as a scientist or a scholar.

As you would be aware, the first session has the mathematics paper which is the difficult one. The second session is after the lunch break and has the easier General Knowledge, Science and English questions. Ensure that you eat a light lunch or snack before the second paper and freshen up before it. Also, leave all thoughts of how you fared in the first paper behind, and attack the new paper with the same fervour as you did the first.

I agree that anxiety exists every time we appear for any test or interview. Therefore, just before the answer sheets and the papers are distributed, close your eyes and meditate for a few minutes to calm your nerves. Deep breathing exercises are very helpful.

Once the question paper booklet is in your hands, do not be in a hurry to start answering. Go through the paper in the first 10 minutes or so. Mark out the questions you are certain of solving with a pencil. Also mark the questions that you do not know at all.

After you have done that, start the paper with positive thoughts. While some of you may mark your answers immediately on the OMR sheet provided, some may note the answer to the question on a rough sheet and put down the answers in the end in one go. Both the methods are fine. Do what you are comfortable with. Just ensure that your answer matches against the correct question number.

I have known of candidates who solved the paper perfectly but marked the answers against the wrong questions! Also, spare OMR sheets are in short supply, so make sure that you do not do mistakes while marking on them.

The exam will soon be behind you and you will be home to rest and recuperate. The answers keys will be available on the internet in a few hours after the exam and you would get a fair idea of how many marks you are going to score. Most of us tend to overestimate our marks when we do this evaluation. In a way, it is good since it keeps you in high spirits as you get on with your SSB training.

For those who have their 12th board exams round the corner, you must change gears to prepare for them. It is important that you do very well in those exams too, so that all optional avenues to join the armed forces remain open. My advice would also be to appear for the JEE/CET or equivalent exams so that you have a backup plan for admission to a good college, in case you do not pass or lose out on merit. Remember, you will have more chances to appear again for the NDA/CDS/AFCAT/NAVCAT. Also, a good score in your JEE/CET can enable you to apply for admission to the armed forces through the Technical Entry Scheme.

For those of you who are still in college, you would be appearing for your CDS/AFCAT just before your final graduation exams. The same advice applies to you all too.

It makes sense to keep all options open; I would like to share one example that comes to mind.

Post passing his NDA written exam, one of my students did not give importance to his class 12 exams and got a poor percentage. Even though he had cleared the SSB interview, he was low in merit and did not get the call letter to join the NDA. He was left high and dry and had to seek admission to a low-end institution which neither did good to his future or to his morale. This boy also lost out on joining through the Technical Entry due to his poor performance in JEE!

In another case, a boy did not pass one subject in his board and his effort at passing the UPSC written exam was wasted!

Therefore, my advice to all youngsters would be to take the last two years at school as well as college, very seriously. Stay focussed and put in your heart and soul into clearing whatever exam you are appearing for. You will not be able to reverse this period, ever. The sacrifices and toil you do at this stage of your life will either make you or break you!

Like it is often quoted in the armed forces: 'The more you sweat in peace, the less you bleed in war!'

What is Personality?

He that fancies himself very enlightened, because he sees the deficiencies of others, may be very ignorant, because he has not studied his own.
—**Edward Bulwer-Lytton**

Personality encompasses the unique and intricate blend of thoughts, emotions, and behaviours that distinguishes one individual from another. This intricate interplay of characteristics arises from a combination of genetic predispositions and environmental influences. Together, they contribute to the character traits in a person.

Examples of one's personality often manifest in the description others have of the person. We might say, 'She is generous, caring, and a bit of a perfectionist,' or 'He is loyal and fiercely protective of his friends.' Such descriptions capture the essence of a person's personality.

The term 'personality' finds its origin in the Latin word 'persona,' denoting the theatrical masks worn by actors to portray the character they are playing. Despite the myriad definitions, most interpretations focus on the distinct patterns of behaviour and attributes that can help predict and explain an individual's conduct.

Explanations for personality variations span a wide spectrum, encompassing genetic predisposition, environmental factors, and personal experiences. All these factors contribute to shaping an individual's character.

So, what are the building blocks of one's personality? It is a composition of enduring traits, cognitive and emotional patterns, and a few fundamental characteristics that define it. These are listed below:

- **Consistency:** Generally, there is a discernible order and regularity to one's behaviour. People tend to act consistently or exhibit similar behaviours across various situations. How you react to a particular stimulus today will be similar to how you did so earlier as well as will do in the future.
- **Psychological and physiological:** While personality is primarily a psychological construct, research suggests that it is also influenced by biological processes and needs.
- **Impact on behaviours and actions:** Personality not only shapes our movement and responses within our environment, but also influences our actions and decisions.
- **Multiple expressions:** Personality manifests itself in more than just behaviour; it extends to our thoughts, emotions, close relationships, and social interactions.

Understanding personality in the Selection Board context

Let us delve into the significance of one's personality in the context of the Selection Board (SSB) evaluation. The SSB scrutinises you to understand who you are at your core. It seeks to uncover the essence of your upbringing, education, and experiences to determine if you possess the attributes necessary for a career in the armed forces.

What makes one unique? In a world where conformity might seem easier, it is our inherent differences that make us individuals. These differences arise from the various life paths, aptitudes, attitudes and distinct neural pathways that shape our behaviour. Even identical twins, raised in the same environment, develop differently unique personalities.

The Oxford Dictionary defines personality as 'The combination of characteristics or qualities that form an individual's distinctive character.' Personality includes enduring traits, interests, drive, values, self-concept, abilities, and emotional patterns. It is who you are as a human being and how others perceive you.

As an aspiring armed forces candidate, you do not need to delve into complex personality theories. Instead, focus on understanding the practical aspects of personality evaluation during your SSB interview.

It is a misconception that the armed forces seek specific stereotypes who conform to a particular type of behaviour. This notion is far from the truth. One cannot fundamentally change your innate traits and force yourself to behave in a specific manner just to suit your job requirements.

What matters in SSB evaluation

So, what matters in the SSB evaluation process? First and foremost, it centres around understanding the nature or content of the job in the armed forces. Once you grasp what the job demands, you can identify the attributes required to excel in it.

For example, if the role calls for leadership, strong social skills become crucial. If physical fitness is paramount, candidates need to demonstrate robust physical health.

Having established the connection between the job content and the necessary attributes, the assessor's task is to evaluate whether you possess these attributes in sufficient measure. This evaluation aligns with the core purpose of the SSB tests.

SSB assessors include a psychologist, the Group Testing Officer (GTO), and the Interviewing Officer (IO), who together scrutinise your inherent qualities against the prerequisites necessary for an armed forces officer. Imagine this as a three-sided prism, with you at the centre. Each assessor observes you through this unique lens, seeking to determine your suitability for the military. The qualities they assess are consistent; only their assessment techniques vary.

Each quality is quantifiable in terms of what is acceptable, borderline, or unacceptable. These gradations are calculated and form the basis of your evaluation. Even candidates with borderline scores receive consideration, with their fate decided during the final conference.

Understanding the SSB evaluation process

Let me elucidate the entire SSB evaluation process with a practical example:

Imagine a cardboard cutout of a human figure kept vertically on a stand. The cutout has holes drilled at various points, each representing a personality trait. The hole cut through the head represents the intelligence of the candidate and the hole near the limb, his physical stamina. When a light source is placed on one side of this cutout, it passes to the other side through these holes. This is the candidate with 100 per cent qualities—an exact match of those required for this job.

Now we have another cutout of the same dimensions without any holes cut in. When this is placed on top to cover the first cutout, no light can pass through it.

Consider this second cutout to be you. After your evaluation, the assessor cuts in the holes in this second cutout according to his evaluation. If you score 70 per cent in, say, your intelligence quotient, he will carve a hole of 70 per cent diameter of the original at the same place on the head. If you score 40 per cent in your physical stamina, the hole will only be 40 per cent of the original. The assessor will, similarly, cut holes of different sizes for each of the attributes he has evaluated you for.

Once this new cutout is placed over the original, it will leave some space (not 100 per cent) for light to pass through. If this total amount of light passing through is measured and found acceptable, you would have deemed to have passed.

This is how SSB evaluations work

Essentially, you yourself determine your success in the SSB process. The SSB starts with every candidate having a score of 100 per cent—similar to the first cutout described. As you are evaluated, your negative marks result in you becoming the second cutout.

Can you train to alter your personality?

A common query is whether one can train to change one's personality to meet the armed forces' requirements. Can professionals help sharpen personality traits to align with these standards? If this was the case, a plethora of trainers would be making substantial incomes, and success rates would be high.

However, a visit to any training academy reveals the stark reality. The percentage of their candidates who pass the SSB still remains relatively low. You cannot alter your personality traits or pretend to be someone you are not.

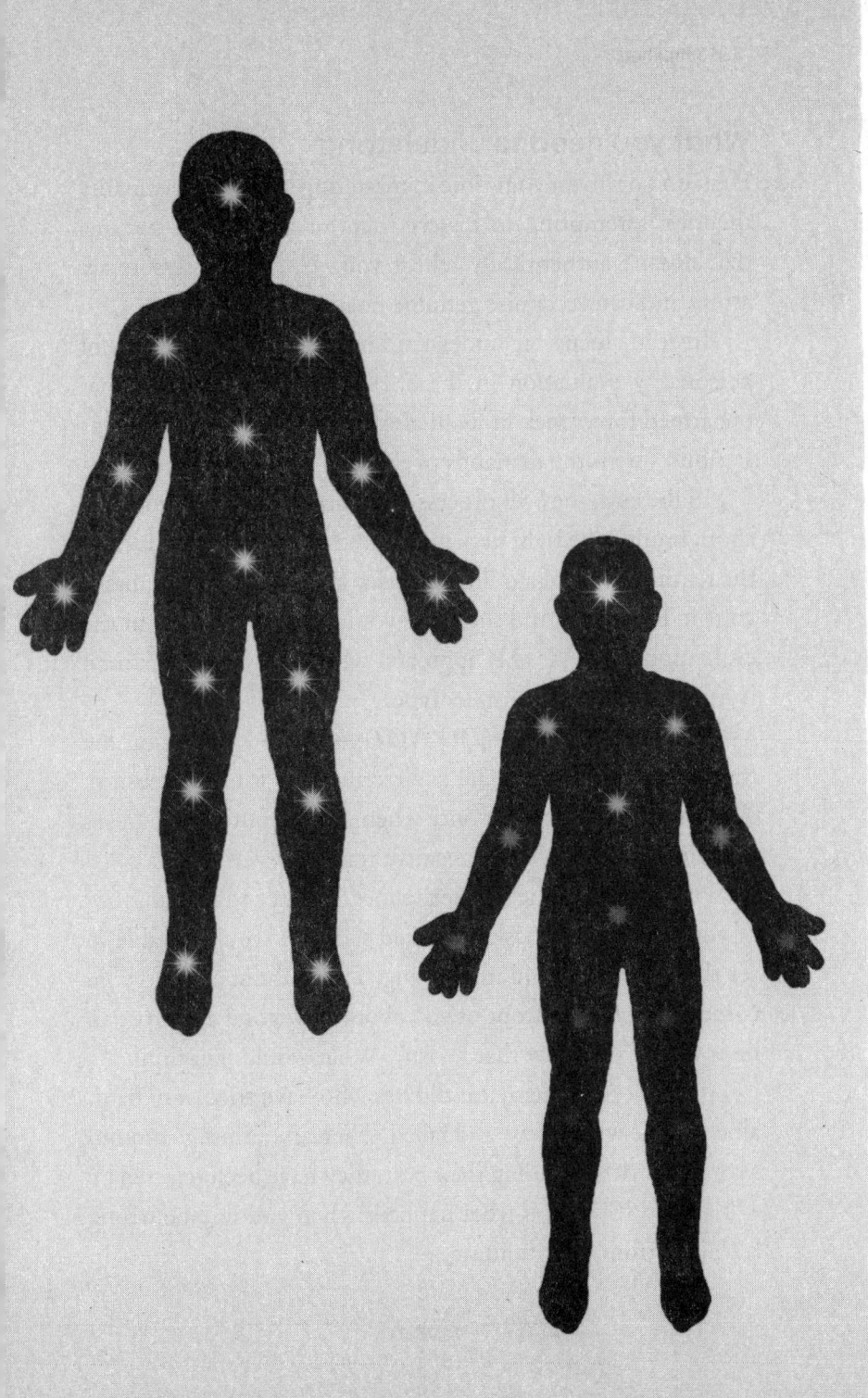

What you need to understand

First, do not invest your time in mastering complex personality theories, attempting to dissect traits or adopting a persona that doesn't authentically reflect you. The SSB assessors are astute and can recognise genuine qualities.

Instead, focus on understanding the practical aspects of personality evaluation in the SSB interview. Recognise that the armed forces seek individuals who can align their inherent attributes with the demands of the job.

In the end, the SSB process is not about changing you, but about finding the right fit between your unique personality and the requirements of a military career, so go ahead and embrace your individuality and showcase your genuine qualities in the evaluation process. This approach will serve you better than trying to conform to a stereotype.

As a final takeaway: **DO NOT** go around emulating the traits of an ideal candidate as described on various websites. The assessor will know at once when you are putting on an act or trying to disguise your negative traits.

Put yourself in the assessor's shoes. If the candidate in front of you is trying to mask his actual self, you would be able to see through it and find it irritating. Think about a friend who comes and brags in front of you about how good a sportsman he is when you know that he isn't. What would you think?

I have seen so many candidates who have tried very hard, albeit in the wrong way, and failed. Thereafter, they go around saying that despite doing their best, they have been rejected by a 'biased' SSB! This is what happens when you imbibe wrong learnings from your training.

✯ ✯ ✯

Preparation for the SSB

> By failing to prepare, you are preparing to fail.
> –Benjamin Franklin

Exam results are now announced in just a few weeks, thanks to the improvement in the technology of electronic and automated checking of the OMR sheets. It has also become faster these days due to another reason. The mathematics paper is checked first and the second paper checked of only those candidates who clear the cut-off marks for mathematics. You must be aware that almost 5 to 7 lakh candidates (a little lesser for exams like AFCAT) appear for the NDA and the CDS written exam, every six months. That is a lot, and you can imagine the logistics of conducting and evaluating an exam on such a large scale.

In any case, if you have prepared well, you should find your name in the list of passed candidates on the website. As I had described in an earlier chapter, titled 'Start Early and Train Best,' the SSB training must now be given priority and attention along with your studies, of course!

It was in 1980 that I went for my SSB. My father had been through his selection to the armed forces in the 1950s and could barely remember what had happened back then, so he really couldn't brief me. His friends weren't of much help either and the only way to find out what actually happened at the SSB was to go there yourself!

The only thing my father advised me then was to practise rope climbing and attempt some of the obstacles present in the training area of his unit. I found it fun to do, little realising that it was toughening me up in the process!

And then, on the day I was leaving for the SSB with butterflies in my stomach, a friend of my father had dropped by to meet our family. I promptly asked him for some last minute advice, just in case he had something different to say. 'Just go out there and enjoy yourself!' he said, wishing me the best. That, I realised later, was one very important piece of advice, and one that remained in my mind forever.

I shall talk more of that later.

After so many years, I do believe that it is the best advice to give to anyone. Just go out there and enjoy the process! It keeps you calm, tension-free and also improves your performance! Try it out when you attempt your SSB!

I am reminded of one of my students at the AFPI whose example will cement what I am saying. Let us call him Mr S for success.

Mr S came from a very small town and from a very modest family; but he was bright in studies. Moreover, he was a keen learner and took his training seriously. He had passed the written exam and whilst he was undergoing SSB-specific training, he suddenly developed cold feet.

One day, he came to my office and confided in me, telling me that he wasn't good enough as the others and felt very underconfident since his spoken English skills were not as good as his friends.

I found out later that his friends were one of the reasons for his negative thoughts. One day, as they discussed the SSB procedure post-dinner, almost all of them told him that he did not stand a chance since he couldn't speak well because of the background he came from.

We had about two months to go for his SSB and I decided to take it upon myself to improve Mr S's confidence level. I told him not to worry about all the other aspects of the SSB and concentrate on his spoken and written skills. We kept doing the exercises I have mentioned in the earlier chapters for the 60-odd days left, at the end of which, I found him fairly acceptable.

A day before he was leaving, I called him for a final briefing on the entire process. He told me that although he felt better about his English now, his confidence levels were still sagging and he needed some last-minute tips to improve them.

I remembered the pep talk my father's friend had given me all those years ago. 'Just go there and enjoy the process,' I said to him. Giving him a pat on his back, I added, 'Remember that all those guys out there are as good or as bad as you; you stand the same chance as each of them to clear the SSB!'

As you would have already realised, Mr S was successful at the SSB and when he returned, he was brimming with confidence.

I made him stand in front of his class and asked him about the secret behind his success. He also prepared a do's and don'ts brief of the selection process for his friends who were about to go for their SSB.

'Sir,' he said, 'you told me to go and enjoy the process and I did just that! I really do not know how I passed!'

For me, personally, it proved one fact that I keep telling

everyone: 'There is no point preparing for each of the tests as they do in training institutes; work on your individual being and polish yourself as a person, and success will be yours!'

These days, almost all aspirants who come for their SSB go in for some kind of training. While many of them don't really benefit from the many shortcuts to success that these training institutes tout, some boys and girls are still able to grasp the essence of what is being taught and are able to value-add to their preparations.

As I have said many times, I hold a different view altogether than the scores of training academies that have mushroomed in every small town and in big cities. For all those who still want to go to the training academy for their short courses, my advice would be to:

First learn the essence of what is being taught;

Second, do not prepare for any test by rote;

And third, do not try the shortcuts that some training academies advocate.

Remember, there are no shortcuts to success in life and none at all at the SSB!

In the next few chapters, we shall learn of each of the tests that you will be going through. For now, I shall reiterate the following:

- Prepare for the screening test (the next chapter deals with this).
- Be physically fit and mentally relaxed.
- Learn the art of speaking well, writing well and listening well; I am sure that most of you do not require expensive training for it. I have already given you tips on how to train for this.

- Know your surroundings well. From the details (history, geography, demographics, etc.) of the place you live in, to the gadgets you use and about what is happening in India and the world, and knowledge of the armed forces, there is so much to just read and know about. If you have started early, you could be well ahead of the class at this time!
- If possible, try and visit an armed forces establishment to get a 'feel' of the life of a soldier.
- Please, *please*, **please** do start reading. It is one of the most important facets of personality development. Over the many years that I have dealt with young aspirants, I have found this to be a major lacuna. Like I explained earlier, reading as a hobby has just too many benefits for you to not do it—even for a good life outside of the armed forces!
- Pick up some games and a hobby or two if you haven't already. Benefits are many and need no emphasis.
- Last but not the least, find out from a reliable person or a trusted website what the SSB is about. You don't need too much detail, but you should be aware of what you will be experiencing in the five days at the Board. This book will also cover the day-wise activities over the next few chapters. If you read this book carefully from end to end, and follow my tips in letter and spirit, you may not need to go to any training institute at all!
- As I have said many times earlier, the best time to start learning is NOW!

The table gives you a brief outline of the five-day process at the SSB:

Day	Activity	Duration	Remarks
Day 1	Arrival formalities	00:45	You may be arriving at some SSBs in the evening
	Checking of documents	00:30	Individual document check 3-5 min per candidate
	Allotment of chest numbers	00:30	
	Opening address	00:15	
	Officer Intelligence Rating test	01:00	Briefing plus two test booklets of 00:20 min each
	Picture Perception and Description Test	1:30-2:00	Depending on total strength. Picture description test for 10 min and discussion for 20 min per batch
	Results-Phase 1	00:15	Unsuccessful candidates go back after departure formalities

	Reallotment of chest numbers	00:15	
	Allotment of rooms/ beds and settling down	00:45	
	Psych test	02:30	In the evening/next morning—may differ from board to board
Day 2	Psych test	02:30	As above
Day 2,3,4	Individual interview	00:45-01:00	
	Group tests in batches of 8-10		For two days per batch, total 8 hours
Day 5	Final Board interview	3:00	3-5 min per candidate
	Announcement of results and departure of unsuccessful candidates	00:45	
	Filling of forms by successful candidates	2:00	
Day 6	CPSS (Old PABT)	2:30	For air force flying branch aspirants only

The SWOT Analysis

Nothing turned as something – Strength
Something turned as nothing – Weakness
Something may be everything – Opportunity
Everything sometimes nothing – Threat
–Kavibharathi Selvan

Over the years, after having interacted with thousands of candidates, I have concluded that an analysis of the self is most important as part of the training for the SSB. Mind you, this is not taught in the curriculum at the training institutes that I spoke about!

Who knows you best? Your mother? Father? Siblings? Teachers?

The answer is '**No**' to all of them. It is '**You**' who knows yourself the best! So why not carry out this exercise by yourself for yourself and learn from it? It is easy enough to do, but you may like to research on the internet to know the basic theory of how such an analysis is done.

Having done that, you will find that it is an easy exercise, but one which needs to be done with utmost sincerity. If you do not, then it will be you who will be going in the wrong direction! So do it for yourself; and you do not have to discuss it with anyone. Keep it as your little secret never to be told! SWOT stands for:

- **Strengths(S)**
- **Weaknesses(W)**
- **Opportunities(O)**
- **Threats(T)**

While this analysis can be applied to almost anything, the most challenging is to apply it to the human being, since the qualities of a human are most intangible. For example, if one does routine problem-solving by this technique, it would be an easy matter.

Say, you need to analyse the strength of a bridge and suggest a subsequent repair strategy using SWOT. With this tool, you could find out what are the strong areas of the bridge, what was the material used during construction, how much load was it made for, how good is the soil and other such details. Thereafter, you could jot down the reasons why the bridge has weakened with time, perhaps due to the water flow, impact of the weather on the steel and concrete and the traffic density etc. Having analysed all aspects, one could arrive at multiple solutions about what needs to be done in the short, medium, and long-term to keep the bridge operational till a more permanent solution (like building a new bridge) is found.

The other reason why I said that it is a difficult exercise to do on human qualities is because all human beings are hardwired to hide or downplay their weaknesses and are boastful about their strengths, thereby taking your analysis in an incorrect direction. That is why this exercise needs to be done alone, with oneself and no one needs to know the outcome except for yourself! So, be truthful while you do this little game to know yourself. It will make for interesting reading later, especially when you revisit it a few years later.

Why do you need to know yourself? The answer is simple really. It will:
- Help you to reach your goals.
- Help in decision making for the future.
- Help in understanding and improving personal relationships.
- Help in improving your overall happiness quotient.
- Help you to understand your emotional quotient, take control of your emotions and take calculated decisions.
- Tell you how to exploit your strengths and provide for success in all areas of life.

The analysis

The SWOT is a part of a critical thinking process. As described earlier, it can be applied to any problem or situation. It is an analytical tool which helps you in problem-solving and in making decisions. It leads to self-discovery and helps you in understanding alternate solutions and choosing the best path for yourself and of course, in quicker decision making.

When we face any problem in life, we generally tend to address the outcomes rather than going to the root cause or source of the problem. We often tend to take life as it comes and move on when the problem is behind us. It is good in a way, but if you are self-aware after carrying out the SWOT, you will have the tools to deal with that problem if it reoccurs.

Also, you would be more analytical about the how and why of the problem and not take knee-jerk decisions. This self-discovery exercise gives you solutions to any problem that you face in life, whether it is academics, your career, or any aspect of your personal life. Once you are familiar with it, it will quickly become your 'go to' tool.

On the flip side, it is recommended that one be careful

while using this analysis and be ready to change course if things do not work out the way you anticipated, and therefore, it is recommended that it be used as a guide only.

Be specific while doing the analysis, and avoid going too much into details. Do not venture into unknown or grey areas. Focus on the situation at hand rather than going into peripherals. In essence, keep the SWOT short and simple!

The following diagrammatic representation will be helpful for you to carry out a SWOT.

The self-description essay

Having gone through the SWOT exercise, it is now time to write a short essay about yourself. You may use the facts gleaned from the SWOT.

Choose a time when you are fresh, perhaps, first thing in the morning to write this essay. Be with yourself, relaxed and without distractions when you attempt this exercise.

In the essay, cover the following areas:
1. Your early life and family background.
2. Your educational profile/journey till date.
3. Where are you headed now, what you need to do or accomplish in the next few years.
4. Describe your relationships with your friends and family. Who are the people that you like and who are the people that you would like to avoid? Who are your best friends and why do you consider them so? Think of other similar questions.
5. What are the hobbies and other interests you have? How do you keep yourself abreast with what is happening in the world today? What is it that you would like to do in the areas of hobbies and other co-curricular interests?
6. What are the qualities within you that make you a unique personality? What areas would you like to improve? Who is your role model and the reason why?
7. Why do you want to join the profession of arms? What is it in the armed forces that interests you the most?
8. How do you see yourself five to ten years from now? What are your alternate career options? Are you working towards them? If so, what are your plans to achieve your secondary career options?

This is not a self-description test as required to be done at the SSB. This is only an essay about yourself to make you more self-aware. However, there is no denying that this will surely help you later at the SSB. Please keep this essay in a safe place if you do not want anyone to know of it; but once in a while, read through it. It will keep you mindful of your strengths and weaknesses.

Besides this, I recommend another exercise that you must undertake. I call it the PIQ-tree. For that, you need to download the PIQ form from the internet and then start doing something with it.

✯ ✯ ✯

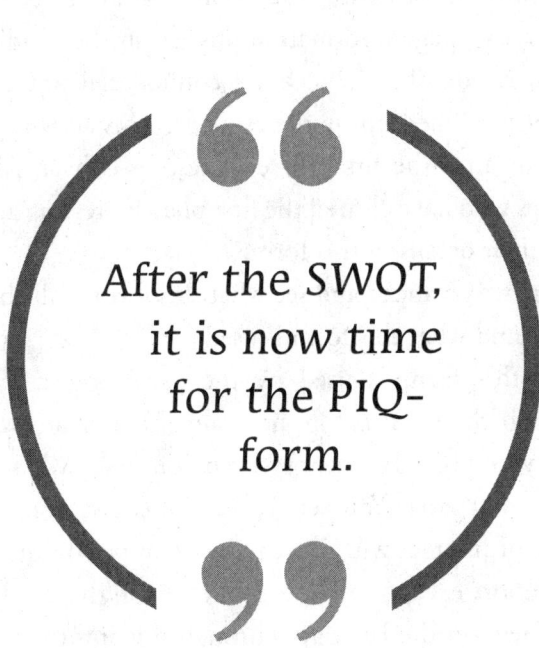

After the SWOT, it is now time for the PIQ-form.

PIQ Form: The Personal Information Questionnaire

> The goal is to turn data into information,
> and information into insight.
> –Oscar Wilde

The Personal Information Questionnaire or 'PIQ' form in short, is a two-page information dossier on the candidate. It stands to reason that it becomes confidential 'information' only after it is filled up by the aspirant! This activity is done at the SSB after the first phase of testing is over. All those candidates who have cleared the first phase of testing are made to fill in their details in this form.

Before we go ahead and see what this form is all about, let us understand what this form is used for.

- First, this form is used by the psychologist. He goes through the form before he evaluates your answer sheet that you filled in the psychological test. We will talk about that later. You see, the psychologist does not get to see or interact with the candidate in person during the evaluation except in the conference or the final Board interview on the last day. Through this information, the psychologist forms a mental image about you; that helps in further evaluation.

- Second, the PIQ form is needed by the Interviewing Officer (IO) for the same reason. The IO will scrutinise this form as well as your certificates before the interview. The information that you provide here will help him in forming questions for the interview. Therefore, it is important that this form is filled in legibly, neatly and with correct information.
- Last but not the least, a copy of this form is kept at the SSB for record.

Therefore, you need to fill this form in triplicate. Before you go for the SSB, you must practice filling this form; the reason for this will be clear when you go through this chapter.

Your handwriting, neatness, and the way you go about filling this form gives the assessors a fair idea of your persona, and therefore, this form is a very important document.

Use a nice free flowing ball-point pen for this purpose. Be aware of what you need to write where, so that you avoid mistakes. Just think, if I were to give you a handwritten note of instructions that is hardly legible and has a lot of overwriting, omissions and spelling mistakes, what impression would you form of me?

Both inadequate or excessive information provided on the PIQ can spell your doom in more ways than you can imagine. Please remember this.

What all is required to be filled in this form? Let us first look at the form. The form is printed on both sides of a single sheet of paper as shown.

Paragraphs 1 to 6 cover information like your name, place of residence, religion, whether you are from a backward class, and information about your parents and siblings.

गोपनीय
CONFIDENTIAL

डी॰ आई॰ पी॰ आर॰ प्रश्नावली संख्या 107-A (संशोधित)
DIPR Questionnaire No. 107-A (Revised)

व्यक्तिगत जानकारी प्रश्नावली
PERSONAL INFORMATION QUESTIONNAIRE

ओ॰ आई॰ आर॰ / **O.I.R.** _____

1.	चयन बोर्ड (संख्या और स्थान) Selection Board (No. & Place)	बैच सं॰ Batch No.	चैस्ट सं॰ Chest No.	यू॰ पी॰ एस॰ सी॰ या अन्य रोल नम्बर UPSC / Other Roll No.

2. सुस्पष्ट अक्षरों में नाम (जैसा मैट्रिक प्रमाण-पत्र में है) / Name in CAPITALS (As in the matriculation certificate) _____

3. पिता का नाम / Father's Name _____

4. (a) अधिकांश समय आवास का स्थान (स्थान, जिला, राज्य) (स्थान की अनुमानित जनसंख्या सहित)
   Place of <u>Maximum Residence</u> (Place, District, State)
   (with approximate population of the place) _____

   (b) वर्तमान आवास का स्थान (स्थान, जिला, राज्य) (स्थान की अनुमानित जनसंख्या सहित)
   Place of <u>Present Residence</u> (Place, District, State)
   (with approximate population of the place) _____

   (c) स्थाई आवास का स्थान (स्थान, जिला, राज्य) (स्थान की अनुमानित जनसंख्या सहित)
   Place of <u>Permanent Residence</u> (Place, District, State)
   (with approximate population of the place) _____

   (वह जिला मुख्यालय है अथवा नहीं) / (Whether District HQ or not) _____

5. निम्न विवरण भरें / Fill in the details below :-

राज्य और जिला State & District	धर्म Religion	अनुसूचित जाति / जनजाति यदि है Whether SC / ST / OBC	मातृ भाषा Mother Tongue	जन्म तिथि Date of Birth	विवाहित / अविवाहित / विधुर Married / Single / Widower

6. (a) क्या माता-पिता जिवित हैं? / Parents Alive   हां/नहीं / Yes / No
   (b) यदि जिवित नहीं तो माता / पिता की मृत्यु के समय आपकी आयु
       If not alive, your age at the time of Mother's / Father's death _____
   (c) माता-पिता/संरक्षक और भाई-बहन के व्यवसाय/आय (जो लागू हो) / Parents' / Guardian's and Siblings' Occupation/income (as applicable) :-

विवरण / Particulars	शिक्षा / Education	व्यवसाय / Occupation	मासिक आय / Income per month
पिता / Father			
माता / Mother			
संरक्षक / Guardian			
बड़ा भाई/बहन / Elder Brother / Sister			
बड़ा भाई/बहन / Elder Brother / Sister			
छोटा भाई/बहन / Younger Brother / Sister			
छोटा भाई/बहन / Younger Brother / Sister			

7. शैक्षिक रिकार्ड (मैट्रिकुलेशन/समकक्ष परिक्षा से आरम्भ करके) / Educational Record (commencing from Matriculation / Equivalent Examination) :-

प्राप्त योग्यताएँ Qualification acquired	संस्थान का पूरा नाम Full Name of Institution	बोर्ड / युनिवर्सिटी Board / University	वर्ष Year	श्रेणी व अंक प्रतिशत / Div. & Marks %	शिक्षा का माध्यम Medium of Instruction	छात्रावासी / दिन छात्र Boarder / Day Scholar	असाधारण उपलब्धि, यदि कोई हो / Outstanding achievement, if any
मैट्रिक / हायर सैकेंडरी Matric / Hr. Sec.							
10+2 के समक्ष 10+2 Equivalent							
स्नातक / Graduation							
स्नातकोत्तर / व्यवसायिक Post-Graduation / Professional							

गोपनीय
CONFIDENTIAL

गोपनीय
CONFIDENTIAL

8. आयु (वर्ष और माह) / Age (Years & Months) _____ उचाई (मीटर में) / Height (in Metre) _____ वजन (किलोग्राम में) / Weight (in Kilogram) _____

9. वर्तमान व्यवसाय और व्यक्तिगत मासिक आय, यदि है
   Present Occupation and personal monthly income, if any _____

10. (a) राष्ट्रीय कैडिट कोर प्रशिक्षण / N.C.C. Training   हां/नहीं / Yes/No
    (b) यदि हाँ, तो कुल प्रशिक्षण (विवरण नीचे दो) / If Yes, Total Training (Give details below)

कुल प्रशिक्षण / Total Training	स्कंध / Wing	प्रभाग / Division	प्राप्त प्रमाण पत्र / Certificate Obtained

11. (a) खेलकूदों में भागीदारी / Participation in games & sports :-

खेल / क्रीड़ा का नाम Games / Sports	भाग लेने की अवधि / Period or duration of Participation	स्कूल/कालेज/विश्वविद्यालय/अन्य जहाँ का प्रतिनिधित्व किया / Represented School / College / University / Other	असाधारण निष्पति, यदि कोई हो Outstanding achievement, if any

(b) शोक/रुचियां / Hobbies / Interest _____
(c) पाठ्य विषयेत्तर सामूहिक कार्यकलापों में भागीदारी / Participation in extra-curricular, activities :-

कार्यकलाप समूह का नाम Name of the activity group	भाग लेने की अवधि / Duration of Participation	असाधारण निष्पति, यदि कोई हो Outstanding achievement, if any

(d) राष्ट्रीय कैडिट कोर/ स्काउटिंग/ खेलकूद/ पाठ्येत्तर और अन्य क्षेत्रों में उत्तरदायित्व का पद
   Position of responsibility/offices held in NCC/Scouting
   Sports Team/Extra-curricular group and other fields _____

12. (a) कमीशन का स्वरूप / Nature of Commission
    (b) सेवा का चयन / Choice of Service

13. तीन सेवाओं में कमीशन के लिए कितने मौके ले चुके हैं -
    Number of chances availed for commission in all three Services _____

14. पिछले सभी साक्षात्कारों का विवरण, यदि कोई हो (आर्मी / नेवी / एयर फोर्स चयन बोर्ड)
    Details of all previous interviews, if any (Army / Navy / Air Force Selection Boards)

क्रम सं• /Sl. No.	प्रवेश का प्रकार जिसके लिए बैठे Type of Entry	एस• एस• बी• नं• और स्थान SSB No. & Place	तारीख / Date	चैस्ट और बैच नं• Chest No. / Batch No.

गोपनीय
CONFIDENTIAL

Paragraph 7 deals with your educational journey. Keep your data for the same handy when you write details about your school-leaving exams.

Paragraph 8 starts on the reverse side of the paper. Here you list your personal details such as age, height, and weight.

Paragraph 9 asks for details of present occupation and income. For most of you reading this, the occupation would read 'Student' and income would be Nil. For those in jobs, this needs to be filled up with actual details.

Paragraph 10 asks you about your experience at the NCC (if any). If you have passed A/B/C certificate exams, mention the grade achieved.

Paragraph 11 is an important part of the PIQ. It asks you to list your participation in games and sports, hobbies and interests including participation in extra-curricular activities and positions of responsibilities held. A lot of candidates are shy of writing this information, while on the other hand, some tend to be boastful.

Find a good dictionary, or from google, find out the difference between Hobbies, Extra Curricular Activities, and Interests. Make a note of what you would like to put down under each column. To write about games and sports is easy, but you must be clear about what needs to go under the other two heads.

For example, you may play football and have it as a hobby, too. You must know what exactly about football will fall under the category of Hobby/Interest.

The next few paragraphs in the form ask you for details of previous SSB appearances, choice of service etc. Write down the choice of service in the order of your priority (Eg., 1. Army, 2. Navy, 3. Air Force) and indicate if you are going in for Permanent Commission or Short Service. As far as the service-specific exams like the AFCAT are concerned, you would have just one choice of service. Some of you may be applying for only short service entry.

If you have appeared for an SSB earlier, please mention the details in the space provided. Fill this column only if you have been screened out in Phase 1 or have been 'Conferenced out' or passed as the case may be. Do not bluff about the chances you have availed at the SSB since your records are available on the database.

The PIQ tree

Having understood what this form is required for, how it is to be filled and how it helps in assessment of the candidate, I devised an exercise from the candidate's point of view. This unique exercise will not only help you at the SSB, but in life as well. So read this carefully. If you follow my instructions, I am confident that this will benefit you immensely during your gruelling tests at the Selection Centre.

I have named this exercise, The PIQ Tree!

Get a new notebook for this exercise. Reserve a few pages each for the various PIQ paragraphs. You could cut the paragraphs from the printout and stick them on the first page of each part. Ideally, it is best to have a notebook into which you can add pages to each section, later if needed.

Once you have this ready, commence your writing.

Write what is asked from you in each of the columns. Once that is done, think of the questions that could be asked from each of these entries and write the answers. From these answers, what are the questions that can be asked, further? Think about them and let this tree grow.

Let us now take a few examples from the PIQ form, itself, to understand this better. The first paragraph asks you to write your name in capitals. What could be asked about your name? Who kept this name? Why was it kept? What is the significance of this name in mythology? For example, if your name is SURAJ, you will say that it means the Sun. This could lead to questions on the Sun, itself. How far away is the Sun? How long does sunlight take to reach the earth? What is the temperature of the Sun? What are the various names for the Sun...the questions on the Sun, itself, can be endless.

From your father's income and profession, what could be asked? Once again, many things. Do it as an exercise and write down what all can be asked about the information you have listed here. For this tree to grow, you will now have to get some details from your father! What does he do really, and how does he do it, for instance.

Now let us analyse the first table that you will fill in at the end of the first page—about your educational journey. The questions that could emanate could centre around the drop in your percentage; what subjects you excelled in; the subject that you liked the most, and so on. What was the type of school you went to? What were the facilities there? What did you like best about the school? What did you not like? The list of questions can be limitless, so make it a point to learn something about your school as well.

Let us take another example. Suppose you have written that cricket is your favourite sport and you have excelled in it at school or college, then what questions can you be asked about cricket? From details of the game, to questions on the world champions, to the distance between the wickets and when and how the game of cricket was invented; to why and how does a ball swing and the physics behind it—these could be just some of the things that could be asked!

Look at the preliminary answers to each of the first questions that occur to you and ask the second and third set of questions to yourself, based on your answer. Jot all this down and watch your tree grow.

By growing your PIQ tree, what exactly is it that you are achieving? You are creating a better understanding of yourself by going into the details of your past which you hitherto had taken for granted.

This is not a one-day exercise. Revisit the book many times so that this tree keeps growing. The more this tree grows, the more your self-awareness grows, as also the awareness of your surroundings. I can guarantee you that!

And when this self-awareness grows, it will lead to improvement of your self-esteem and confidence, both of which are required in good measure at the SSB. Rest assured, this has more positive outcomes than you can imagine.

Having carried out this exercise with several of my students, I can assure you that this will pay rich dividends.

★★★

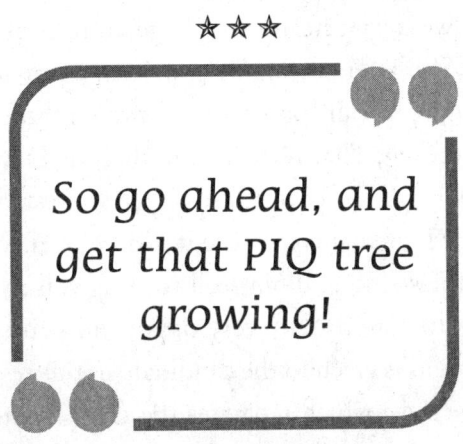

So go ahead, and get that PIQ tree growing!

Day 1 at the SSB: Sifting the Chaff From the Grain

Opportunities do not happen, you create them.
–Chris Grosser

Day One at the SSB is the most crucial, because on the basis of this day, you must make it to Phase-2 of the testing to go through to the real SSB. If you are prepared well, let me assure you that getting through Phase-1 is not difficult. You may have done very well in the written exam, but if you do not do well on the first day, then all your efforts will go down the drain. Therefore, we need to understand the concept of the screening test and prepare well for it.

Why do we call it screening? A large number of candidates come to the SSB after passing their written exam and it is not humanly and logistically possible to put them through the full five days of testing. That is the reason that the Day 1 test was designed. During this set of tests, we try and establish if you have the basic ingredients to make it to an officer. We are only looking for the sparks and not really testing you at this stage.

It stands to reason that every opportunity, including the benefit of doubt, is given to the candidate in this test. This test is like a large sieve which separates the chaff from the grain.

Many candidates have a fear psychosis of getting through this first phase, itself. Even if it is a repeat of what I have said earlier, let me reiterate that this test is NOT difficult if one is trained correctly. We shall cover this test in detail in this chapter.

Why do I reiterate the phrase, 'train correctly?' Going by my experience at the SSB of sifting through a large number of candidates, I realised that some of the coaching centres and institutes do a shoddy job of training candidates for this test. The fear psychosis is also built up in the candidates during this training, leading to their failure. You will understand better as we go along this chapter.

Let's start at the beginning. Let's assume that you have received the call letter and are preparing to leave for the SSB centre.

The journey and arrival at the SSB

Go through the call letter for the SSB, which would have arrived by email. I advise you to go through this email diligently to save yourself some last-minute embarrassment. And if you still have doubts, despite going through the instructions carefully, then there is a helpline number for clarifications.

Prepare yourself with your kit for the SSB well in time. If you are getting new formal clothes to wear for the interview, see that they fit you well and that you are comfortable in them, especially in new shoes! I would advise you to wear your new attire a couple of times and then get them ready for the tests; and that includes your track pants or shorts, tee shirts and running shoes, too. Well-fitting clothes make you comfortable and confident at the same time.

Book your journey tickets well in time and ensure that you arrive at the place of the SSB tests at least one day earlier.

Do not rely on the performance of our railways and leave some margin for delays and disruptions. I have known of candidates who arrive literally in their pyjamas to the testing centre straight from the train and present a poor picture of themselves right at the start. Moreover, they are uncomfortable themselves, due to the stress of the journey undertaken. I have also known of candidates who arrived a couple of hours late to the venue and had to be turned back. All this also reflects how badly the candidate wants to join the armed forces!

Remember to keep your tickets after the journey to claim your travel expenses. Keep a copy with you on your mobile if required. You will be paid for the journey at the time of departure.

Take up a room for the night and you may end up meeting a few of your batch mates as you look around town. Make sure that you eat early and get a good night's rest since the next few days are going to be stressful. Get dressed in clothes that are neither overly casual or revealing and reach the SSB or alighting place as mentioned in the call letter. You must look presentable, clean and neat, with a dab of mild fragrance or aftershave as the case may be. This will add to your confidence. Ensure that you have all the things required for the first day's testing ready.

When you arrive at the SSB in buses or at the gate, the luggage will be kept in a secure corner and you will not have access to it till the first phase of testing is over. So, make sure that you have everything that is needed for the first day—your documents, some writing material, identity cards and the call letter.

Some SSBs may ask you to report in the late afternoon, but essentially follow a similar timetable as outlined in the table in this chapter.

I would advise that you keep your watch and other electronics inside your bag as soon as you arrive at the SSB. You may like to give a quick call to your near and dear ones to get their blessings on the phone before you keep it away. Even a wristwatch is not allowed to be worn during the phase 1 testing (PP&DT). So, rather than leave it lying outside the testing rooms, it is better that it is kept secure inside your bag.

You can, of course, call your families once you pass your phase 1. Then, it gets deposited with the security staff for the next five days. You may find that it is a different kind of world when you live without a mobile! Have you ever imagined a world without that gadget? Well, this time, you will find out firsthand! I can assure you that this experience, too, is good.

Another advise that I have for you is to keep a list of important phone numbers with you in a small diary. You will get an opportunity to go outside for an evening during your stay and could find a phone booth to inform your parents, loved ones and friends about how you are faring. You may also get a chance to call up your folks to tell them about what all is happening with you from the local STD booth inside the SSB centre as and when you get time in the evenings.

Now that you are all fresh and ready to take the tests on the first day, let me take you through each of the activities that will take place after you arrive.

The arrival formalities

All the candidates are made to congregate in the open or under a shed depending on the weather. Names are called out and identities established. Bibs or chest numbers, as they are called, are now given to you. Hereafter, you will be called only by your chest number all through the testing process.

The candidates will now line up for the document check. You will be directed to meet officers, who will be seated at tables where you will show your documents, so that your date of birth, documents pertaining to school, mark sheets etc., will be checked. Please make sure that you have all the documents asked for in the joining instructions in a neat folder with additional Xerox copies should you need them later.

As you complete the arrival formalities, you will be given refreshments and get a much needed breather before things start moving at a rapid pace.

Those candidates who have issues with their documents or are not in possession of these documents will be given a fresh date and sent back. For minor requirements which can be met through an email or FAX, candidates will be asked to call up their parents or guardians for them. Once this process is complete, the candidates will move to an auditorium where the President or the Vice-President of the Board will give his opening address.

This done, the formal part of the first day testing will begin.

Test - 1 Officer Intelligence Rating (OIR) Test

This is a simple test of your mental faculty and ability for logic. The test classifies the candidate according to his basic 'intelligence.' What you should know is that the marks obtained in these tests will be only used for your selection on day 1.

To do well, go with a happy state of mind and be confident. After all, you have already passed a far more rigorous exam to reach here, so this is relatively easy. The intelligence test comprises of a verbal test which includes analogy and classification, coding and decoding, number series, puzzles and basic mathematical aptitude which makes it interesting and enjoyable.

The non-verbal part of the test includes analogy and classification of figures, completing patterns, cubes and dice, simple Venn Diagram and motion and analysis etc. You could read about this on the internet and check out some sample questions and practice tests.

The test is for forty minutes and distributed in two booklets containing fifty to sixty questions each. The answers are to be annotated on the printed sheet provided. No rough sheets are given since the calculations are elementary and you won't require paper. You will see that some of the question booklets have markings on them left by some irresponsible candidates. Disregard these as they may not be correct! Please do not deface the question booklets and leave more markings from your side.

As you finish the first booklet at the end of twenty minutes, you will exchange your booklet with the candidate sitting beside you. At the end of forty minutes, it is pens down, and the answer sheets as well as booklets will be taken back from you.

This marks the end of the OIR test and you will now get some time to bond with your new friends whilst the assessors check your answers and collate the marks.

Test - 2: Picture Perception and Description Test (PP&DT)

The PP&DT is an interesting exercise and consists of two parts. First, is the story writing part (picture perception) followed by the group discussion (DT) on it.

You will be made to sit in a large room according to your chest numbers and the psychologist will commence a detailed briefing on the conduct of the test. The test just takes about five minutes and involves writing a story. Listen to the instructions carefully and if you have any doubts, please clear them before the test starts. Doubts will not be entertained once the test commences.

This test requires you to see a picture on the screen (thirty seconds) and write a short story on it in four minutes) which includes details like how many people you saw, their sex, approximate age and mood and what was happening in the picture. The main story will include what led to the situation that you saw in the picture and what was the outcome. It is an exercise of perception, imagination and logical thinking!

When you see the picture on the screen for thirty seconds, please do not be in a hurry to start writing about it as soon as you see it. Observe the picture carefully for the time allotted and let it sink in. Try and observe the minute details in the background too. Think of what could be happening in the picture. The more facts and details of the picture that you observe, the better the story that you will weave around it. Try it out at home yourself. Anything perceived through the visual senses triggers the brain to think and relate to its context almost immediately.

My observations on candidates appearing for this test are that a considerable number of them do not observe the picture for the time allotted, but begin writing immediately. Please understand that thirty seconds are given to you to observe the picture carefully, so make full use of the time. The more you observe, the more the details will be etched in your mind and will emerge as you write your story. A keen observer is able to see many more things and will, therefore, weave a better story around the details.

To observe the picture, see the whole frame first. What all do you see? What is the most striking thing in the picture?

Now concentrate on parts of the picture looking for details and small things in the foreground/background and see how they are related to what is happening in the picture. Again look at the complete picture in the last few seconds and get a good feel of it before it goes off. Now you will be ready to start writing.

Let us take an example of a picture.

Observe the picture for thirty seconds and close the book. What all did you see?

1. A cyclist has been hit by a bus; he is taking a tumble in the air.
2. The bus appears to be on a narrow road, perhaps on a bridge.
3. There is a couple on a scooter just parallel to the boy's cycle.
4. Two more pedestrians are walking on the walkway just behind.

As you observe more closely, what all details do you see?

1. Books belonging to the accident victim flying implying that he could be a student or teacher.
2. Bus has No. 5 with Red Fort written on it.
3. There seems to be some hilly area in the background.
4. The bus appears to be full and the expression of the driver and the co-driver can be seen.
5. The rear end of the cycle seems to be bent.
6. There seems to be a broad footpath on one side where the two people are walking.
7. The scooter seems to be an old kind of model.
8. The couple on the scooter appear to be well dressed. The lady had a fancy hairdo.
9. The cycle seems to be a ladies model.

Many of you would see or perceive even more details in the picture. That is fine. You need to observe the picture as carefully as possible. No doubt, the picture may be hazy, but once you look closely, you will observe more and more details.

The more you observe, the more you will relate to what has happened in the picture.

What will the story be about? Of course, the accident. Whose accident—a boy on a cycle with books. Is he a student or a teacher?

Who all were around? The bus driver and all those inside the bus, the couple on the scooter, the two men on the walkway. What could have happened thereafter?

The boy would be injured slightly or more severely. The traffic would have stopped. A lot of people would have come to help. The scooter couple and the two men on the footpath could be the first responders. The bus driver and other passengers in the bus could have also come out to help. Someone would have called the ambulance and the police. Someone would have cleared the accident site and allowed the traffic to resume later. All these are perceptions based on what all you have been able to see. The more details you see, the more ideas will be generated to make your story cohesive, interesting, meaningful and appropriate.

During your testing, after the picture goes off, you must first mark the characters you saw in the rectangular window provided on the sheet to represent the screen that you just saw. Mark their sex, age and mood in the symbols that will be told to you. (Age is recorded in numbers, sex as M or F and mood in terms of + or -).

If, by this time, some story has formed in your mind, you could write the title in the space provided. If not, you can write the title later.

Put your mind and heart into what you write. It should be nice, original, unique, and a complete story of the picture using the pointers from your observation and linking them up with some imagination. In the thousands of picture perception tests that I have evaluated, I have observed that many of the candidates come for the test with a pre-conceived story in mind and bend what they see in the picture to suit this story; that is **not** to be done!

When you write a preconceived story, it shows that you lack originality and thinking power. Moreover, your story will not be coherent as it may not relate to what you have seen. When you go in for the discussion, you yourself will be uncomfortable since you tried to 'cheat' the system; all this is clearly observed by the assessors. If you are a candidate who has the brains to pass a difficult written exam, I am sure that you have your wits and intelligence about you to write an original story.

Let me divulge important tips about story writing. I have seen how training centres and academies train prospective candidates for this test. For some inexplicable reason, it is often drilled into candidates that their story must revolve around a positive social activity or somehow relate to the armed forces. This is far from the truth and is not required. We are not looking for parrots trained to say just what is taught, but are looking for people who have originality, a logical thinking brain and the language to express what was *seen* in the picture.

This reminds me of a story which my instructors told me when I learnt the art of personality assessment. It was about the boy who only knew how to write an essay on 'The Cow.' Whatever essay topic was to be written about in the exam, he would somehow turn the topic to that of the cow! We certainly do not want people like this in the armed forces!

How does one then prepare for such a test? Simple. Start practising writing. The best way is to follow logic.

Sit with your stopwatch on in your mobile. Look at any picture which has a few characters and a scene, maybe in a book, magazine, or in any media. Look at it for thirty seconds and then time out your story writing. Do this exercise with a group of friends, then discuss the story after each of you have written it. Each person will have a different take on the picture. Everyone's perception is different and, therefore, the stories will be different.

I have heard that many candidates are 'trained' to write a 'positive' story. This is incorrect. Let your story be practical, achievable, and logical; that is all. The picture should be able to tickle your mind to write something on your own rather than twist the tale to fit a preconceived story that you have practised, such as the cow story!

Remember to keep your thinking mind open for this exercise.

Think of your mind like a parachute. It works best when open!

The Discussion Test

As soon as you finish writing, the paper will be folded and you will be asked to keep it in your hand for the second part of the exercise, which begins almost immediately. You will be split into groups of eight to ten (sometimes a few more) and taken to a room for story narration and discussion where three assessors will be present.

The discussion test generally lasts for about twenty to twenty-five minutes and involves narration of the story by each candidate followed by a group discussion.

There will be many groups formed among the candidates and, therefore, you may get some time to think before your group is called in. If I was you, awaiting my group's turn, I would quietly close my eyes, and think about how I am going to narrate my story. Mental preparation will surely help in your narration.

And yes, even if you have the paper on which you wrote the story, you are not allowed to read it or refer to it while you wait. I remember once when I was president of the SSB, while walking to a class to conduct the discussion test, I noticed a few boys going through their story discreetly. We had no choice but to withdraw the candidates for using unfair means. You must appreciate that reading from your script would put you at an unfair advantage, and obviously, is discouraged.

Let's return to the discussion room. You will be made to sit in a semicircle according to your chest numbers. You will not be allowed to take writing material, pens, watch or wallet inside for the test. It will be just you and the folded sheet of paper! That paper in your hand will give you the confidence that your story is with you! After the test is over, the sheets will be collected by the assessors. As soon as you settle down in your seats, the Group Testing Officer (GTO) will commence the briefing.

He will brief you about the maximum time and the order of narration (according to your chest numbers), the discussion format and the consensus story that the group needs to put out, at the end. Once this briefing is done, you would be asked if you have any doubts and now is the time to clear them, if you have any. Thereafter, the test will commence.

At the end of the discussion, which, is usually terminated by the assessor, the group will have to select one of the candidates to narrate the consensus story. The test then ends and you will be asked to deposit your written material and leave the room. The one who narrates the story does not get any additional marks or necessarily gets selected!

As an aide-memoire, some of the points that you need to remember about this narration and discussion test are given below:

- Remain calm and collected; rehearse the narration as you wait for your turn and not while the narration is going on!
- Speak only about what you have written. Do not spice up the story with additional inputs while you speak.
- Speak clearly and slowly so that others can hear you. Do not speak with an accent which is not yours. Use simple language.
- You need not try and impress the assessors by addressing them or looking at them while speaking. Speak to the rest of the members of your group as you would when discussing an issue in a classroom or cafeteria.
- This test also assesses your listening ability. While the others narrate their story, please listen carefully since you will get a lot of ideas and cues to speak on when the discussion starts.

Remember, the discussion phase commences as soon as the last person in the group finishes his narration. If you are in a repeater group, all hell will break loose once the last narration ends and the scene may be described by some as a fish market! Remain calm and do not shout above the others. Look for an opportunity and interject at an opportune moment to put across a point which has substance.

Besides these points that must be kept in mind for the narration phase, some more pertinent points are listed here:

- Don't speak for the sake of speaking and prevent others from speaking. I have seen so many discussions where most of the time was spent on discussing how many people there were, their age, sex, and mood! Instead get to the meat—the main story rather than create a discussion for discussion's sake.
- Try and give some 'solid' points rather than beating about the bush; a person with poor thinking ability will engage in frivolous conversation and waste precious time.
- Allow others to speak, appreciate others' points of view and indulge in healthy discussion rather than trying to impress the assessors. Let them do their job; *do not* bother about them.
- Be courteous, and do not shout to be heard. You will see for yourself, that the candidate who speaks sense will automatically be heard and appreciated by the group. Often, he would be the one chosen in the end to narrate the common consensus story. I have seen so many 'trained' candidates who come and take over the proceedings, yet fail to make an impact. Remember, just a few sentences that matter will help you pass rather than meaningless banter.
- I have met many candidates who get weeded out in the first phase who say that they did very well and yet were not selected. If you follow the thumb rules as given above, no assessor in the world will stop you from clearing this phase.
- Some of you may take time to open up and speak. You keep thinking how to get into the conversation and finally lose the opportunity to speak at all. I have seen many good candidates getting weeded out even though they were of good calibre, just because of this hesitation in speaking up.
- For those going for repeat SSB (repeater batch), you will see a different kind of atmosphere in the discussion room.

Since everyone thinks that he has been weeded out the first time because he spoke less, everyone jumps into the fray, talking at the same time and leading to utter chaos. Such a shouting match makes the atmosphere like a fish market, as I said earlier; in such a case, the assessor may stop the discussion to bring in some order. In some cases, where even order does not prevail, he may be forced to split the group into two to continue with the test.

If I must sum up what you need to do to prepare for the PP&DT, I would say that one needs to start practising writing, speaking, and using your common sense well before the SSB! This can be done by making groups with other aspiring friends and doing mock exercises. If you go down to a training institute, they will make you do a few practise sessions, and while doing that, try and learn the way to go about the exercise rather than attempting to project a wrong image of yourself as many tell you to do.

When you understand what I have said here in this chapter, you will realise that you need to be just a normal human being who is compassionate and just, has a thinking mind, and thinks of the whole group rather than only for himself and does not tread on other people's toes in pursuit of success. What do you think?

The results and after Day 1

After you finish your PP&DT, all of you will be waiting for the others to finish theirs. Once all tests are completed, the assessors will compile the results and announce them.

After the chest numbers of successful candidates are announced, it is time for the ones who have not made it to collect their luggage and leave in the waiting transport for the bus/railway station. Before that happens, these candidates will be given their traveling allowance and complete their departure formalities.

The successful candidates (and I am sure you are going to be one among them) will now be herded together and briefed for the next phase of testing. You will now be given fresh chest numbers and you will be expected to wear these all through your stay at the SSB, except, of course, when you are asleep!

The rooms will be allotted according to the group you are in and you will soon settle down and be ready for the next day's programme which shall be put up on the notice board. This is a good time to get to know your fellow candidates over an outdoor game in the evening or at the dining table.

Walk around the campus, and see the various motivational and informational charts and photos that have been put up. It will give you a flavour of the services as well as help in brushing up on some general knowledge of equipment, men, wars, rank structures, uniforms and more.

There will be candidates who would tell you about the tests in the offing and how they have prepared and what has been told to them at the various coaching institutes. My advice is not to pay heed to such half-baked information, but focus on what *you* have prepared for the days ahead. You may also come across candidates who will brag about knowing how things work at the SSB and end up making you even more sceptical and worried. Take their words with a pinch of salt and don't let it dent your confidence or performance.

Be polite and listen, but disregard what people are saying about what is going to happen. More importantly, **do not** let it affect you in any way.

This is also a good time to bond with your roommates and your group as they will be with you in the GTO tests. You are going to be a team in this test and it is always good to form a rapport with your fellow players. Remember, there is no competition among your peers. All of you are equals in this game.

Your fellow candidates would have come from different places, from different backgrounds and will display different behaviours and reactions. Learn to accept them as your comrades and find out whatever you can about each other in the conversations you have with them.

A word of caution. There will be many out there who will try and influence others about the GTO test and what needs to be done in the tests. Do not fall for this at all. Face the test fresh and without any bias.

With my experience of the SSB, I am aware that a certain amount of pre-planning for the tests takes place before you come face-to-face with the GTO. For example, some of you will try and pre-decide who will call whom for the Command Task so that all get an equal opportunity to help each other. Some candidates decide in advance about who will carry the critical loads and the helping material in the Group tasks and things like that. All this pre-planning and plotting gets thrown out of the window when the tests start! My advice is to not indulge in this unnecessary preparation as it will lead to problems and confusion on the ground the next day.

As an example, suppose you decide beforehand on who is going to be your helper for your command task. But the next day, when you are actually confronting your task, you may realise that the person is not right for the task. This will unsettle you for no reason. Similarly, for the other group tests, once you all see the task in front of you, the plan will emerge on its own from all of you thinking members and the group will automatically decide on who will take on what sub-task.

No amount of pre-planning has ever worked, I can assure you.

The Mess: Your home for the next few days

As you settle down in the new environment, you will realise that your place of residence gives you a feel of an Officers' Mess of the armed forces. It has all the facilities you can think of. The ante-room has the usual TV and some reading material and is a place to relax and interact. There is generally a pool table and a table tennis table, besides many indoor games for your recreation. Outdoor games like basketball, volleyball and badminton are also available.

What these facilities end up doing is to make you understand each other better, make strong bonds (sometimes for life) and, also to enjoy the entire experience of the SSB. I did my SSB so long ago, but the bonhomie and friendship I still share with some of the friends, I made back then, is unbelievable.

A candidate once asked me in the interview if the other staff at the SSB are briefed on observing candidates inside the mess area, when they are eating or playing. I was both amused and aghast at this question. The rumour goes that your general behaviour is under scrutiny by the staff on duty and that there are security cameras all over! This is utter nonsense and should be disregarded.

Just remember to be at your best behaviour, follow rules and restrictions and do not get into arguments or altercations with the staff. If you have a problem, do not hesitate to approach the staff available. The duty officer of the day will meet you before the work for the day commences, just after your breakfast, and at the end of the day after your dinner. You can point out issues or problems to him and he shall sort them out.

At the end of day one, you will start feeling that you have been at the SSB campus for ever! It is finally time to have a good night's rest and be ready for the Psychological Test or Psych Test to be held the next day. This test may be held on the first evening itself at some SSBs, depending on the time available.

> Logic, quick thinking and sound reasoning will get you past the Psych test on Day Two!

The Psychological Test

Answer appears when the problem is clear.
–Keith W Henline

If I had to choose the easiest and least stressful test at the SSB, I would surely name the Psychological Test. All you need here is a quick mind, thinking prowess, writing skills and power of observation and understanding. For this two-and-a-half-hour test conducted first for all candidates together, all you need is a pen which writes well and a mind which is calm.

The Psych test is a set of psychological tests aimed at discerning your personality. How the psychologist goes about doing his job is not our concern, but we must know what is going to happen in this test.

The following are the subtests that you will encounter in this part of the SSB testing. We shall discuss each, with examples.

o   Thematic Apperception Test or TAT
o   Word Association Test or WAT
o   Situation Reaction Test or SRT
o   Self-Description Test or the SDT

First, understand what is required to be done under each test. Once you do that, you need not go through numerous 'practice' tests to hone your skills. Several training academies make you do these in large measure, and in my opinion, this is not required at all. What we need from you here are spontaneous answers, not 'tailored' or 'learnt' answers. For your own good, do not doubt the professional competency of the assessor and make any attempt to hoodwink the system.

As soon as the psychologist scans through your written answers, he can discern or sift the genuine responses from the fake ones. This can become the starting point of a candidate's downfall. In any case, as you run against time answering questions in your test, the stress factor increases and one cannot think of a trained response. Eventually, your genuine responses will come faster and naturally and this is exactly what the psychologist wants. Your responses provide the testing officer 'clues' to your personality. The psychologist is trained, and he will know when to reject the 'trained' responses. He will then be forced to analyse you from the fewer 'genuine' responses, which is not a good thing to happen.

Some points to keep in mind while attempting this test:
- Take writing material which does not smudge.
- Write legibly and neatly.
- Cross outs/overwriting convey a fidgety mind. Avoid this as much as possible.
- Be attentive, and do not panic. Even if a word or sentence is missed out, do not worry.
- There is no minimum and maximum number of responses required to pass. It is about **what you write** rather than **how much you write** which makes you pass or fail in this test. Another misconception that candidates have is

that all responses must have positivity about them. SSB expects you to write your natural responses when an input is given. Therefore, ***do not*** try to step into the shoes of the psychologist and analyse your own response. Let him do his job while you do yours.

At most centres, the test is administered in the morning when you are fresh and you are briefed by the psychologist before the test starts. This is also the time when you can clear your doubts because no questions are allowed during the test. Once the test commences, there will be no breaks between the subtests and your pens will only stop writing at the end of the two-and-a-half hours allotted for this test.

Let us talk about each of the tests in detail.

The Thematic Apperception Test (TAT)

This TAT psychological test uses a series of picture cards to evaluate a person's personality, thought patterns and emotional responses. Each of us have our own perceptions of what we see based on our upbringing, knowledge, state of mind and past experiences.

The TAT takes you through a short story writing spree in which you are supposed to observe a picture for thirty seconds and write a short story on it in four minutes. The pictures keep coming on the screen with a beep sound (from the computer) after a gap of every four minutes and thirty seconds. Keep a track of the sound that will be an indication for you to look at the screen on which a new picture will be flashed.

There are a set of twelve pictures which form this test. Of these, eleven pictures will be hazy and will depict some action scene that will spur your mind to think of a story just like the one you went through on Day - 1 of the testing in PP&DT. The only difference here is that you will not be required to give the age, sex, mood, and the number of characters you saw on the screen. You have to immediately write the story that comes to mind in the four minutes allotted.

The twelfth and last picture is a blank slide. You can think of writing any fictional story that comes to your mind when you see the blank screen. In my experience, one ends up writing the best story on this slide! This is because you can let your imagination run wild in this one!

You will be constantly stressed for time in this test, but if you have been practising writing, then four minutes is a long enough time to write the 150 to 200 words that are required to be written. Also, as you go from one picture slide to the next, you will get engrossed in your thinking and writing, and the stress will be left behind!

Some points to keep in mind about this test:
- There are no extra marks for high end language skills. Use simple language.
- Observe the picture carefully in the time given and note down (in your mind) as many details as possible. Do not be in a hurry to start writing. The more you observe, the more points you will have for your story and the more your imagination will work to weave a story about what you see on the screen.
- Do not go with pre-conceived stories in your head and try to retro-fit them into the picture shown. Use your imagination and thinking ability to write an interesting story.
- Some people may tell you that all the stories need to be positive. They are trying to play with your originality, so

it is best to write about what comes to your mind rather than trying to give a positive twist every time.

- With my years at the SSB, I observed that there is a tendency among the candidates to link each story to the military and 'militariness' and write about war or a related theme. Do not template each story on the life in the armed forces. It is not expected that a person from 'Civvy Street' is so obsessed with the armed forces that he is already in uniform, breathing, eating, living, and even 'writing' in a soldierly fashion!
- Do not carry over the previous story into the next one. Use your creativity to describe the new picture. It should excite you as well.
- If you can't do a particular story well, leave that story behind as you get to the next one. I have met so many candidates who get flustered and stressed when they are unable to complete a story or write what they want to, and end up messing up the other ones. Please avoid this at all costs. What has gone behind, cannot be retrieved, so look forward, keep calm and write the next story better.
- A lot of candidates name their characters Rahul, Raju, Ram, Shyam, Sita, Gita etc. Try and think of the names of your many friends and spin the stories around them instead of these commonly used names. It shows lack of thinking prowess and imagination if you use such run-of-the-mill names!
- Remember, the meat is in the main part of the story which brings out what has happened and the future course of action and the ending, of course. Make sure that you do not waste time writing about infructuous things that are unrelated to the picture or your story.

- You may ask if there is a correct way to write a story? Let me ask you a counter question here: What can you tell me about yourself? How would you start? Think about what is the right way to do that.
- Logically, you will begin by introducing the subject; this will become your introduction. What was shown in the picture? How many characters did you see? Who was the main character in your perception and what was he or she doing?
- The second part of the story brings out the situation depicted and how it happened and what happened after that till the situation ended.
- End the story with a closing sentence (closure) and do not leave a sentence halfway. Give yourself at least thirty-odd seconds to write the ending well.

As soon as this test is over, the Word Association Test (WAT) starts.

The Word Association Test (WAT)

You would have often played some games of this kind. If I show you a word, an image, word or sentence forms immediately in your mind that is associated with the word.

Word association tests your imagination, thoughts, and ideas. These spontaneous thoughts and ideas generated due to the word lead to an understanding of your personality. But as I have already said many times over, we need not think of how the interpretation is done; just be aware what this test is going to be like.

Learn to hone your thoughts, improve your speed of writing, and visualise how much time you will get between the words. Practice for this while preparing for the SSB. Put each of the words in a slide show format and programme the show so that the slide changes every fifteen seconds. If you may plan this test with a group of friends who are also preparing for SSB, it will become a fun activity. A good idea would be to ask a third person to create this test for you.

Some of the trainers may ask you to practice this test and write only positive answers to try and impress the psychologist; let me assure you that this is clearly noticeable to the evaluator and it won't help in any way to mask your answers.

You will be shown sixty words which will be flashed on the screen at an interval of fifteen seconds. After seeing the word, you are expected to write the first thing that comes to your mind in a sentence or in a word or two. If you are spontaneous and your mind is calm, then, the fifteen seconds allotted is adequate time to answer properly. This exercise is about what you write and not the number of answers you give that matters. Keep that in mind while you attempt this test.

The words shown are simple and we use them on a day-to-day basis. This is not a test of your language skills and, therefore, don't be overawed; write what comes to your mind without thinking of using complicated words that might require the use of the dictionary!

The test, like any other, tends to stress you out, especially if you do not manage your time well or over-think before you answer. The stress may also lead to your mind getting muddled or flustered. Remain calm and in case you miss a word or two, it does not really matter.

Remember to be neat and avoid writing illegibly or overwriting over your responses. You do not have to write the word shown, just your answer in the space provided. Neither do you have to use the word in the sentence you jot down. Some candidates tend to write idioms, proverbs, quotes, or phrases in their response to what they see on the screen.

For example, if the word 'Child' is shown on the slide, one may write 'Child is the father of man'. However, avoid such responses as far as possible and steer clear of clichés, as well.

As you come to the end of this test, it will be time for the Situation Reaction Test or the SRT in short.

Situation Reaction Test (SRT)

You will now be given a booklet containing sixty situations. These are day-to-day simple problems one is likely to face. You have to 'React' and write down your immediate thought as you understand the situation.

Your reaction is to be written in a few words or sentences as you deem fit. You need not follow correct English or make long sentences, but it is important that you record your reaction/action/point of view. Even if you write in point form, it is fine, so long as it can be understood by the evaluator.

You will have thirty minutes to answer sixty situations. That gives you about thirty seconds to read and react to the situation posed to you. If your mind is alert and you can think clearly, this test is a piece of cake.

Many a time, I have come across candidates who say that they could attempt only half or three-quarters of the sixty questions. I believe this happens because candidates get flustered when running against time and cannot think clearly or logically to write their reactions in the time available.

Let us take a typical SRT situation:

You are traveling in a train and are in the upper berth of an AC compartment. Suddenly, you hear some commotion in the corridor and through the gap in the curtains you see that there are about four or five stick-wielding goondas who are trying to rob people of their belongings. What would you do?

A few more situations could be:
- You are on a boat cruise when you see that a child has fallen overboard into the water. You do not know swimming very well. What would you do?
- He was riding your bike on a busy street. A dog runs across the street with a lady trying to control him on his leash. His motorcycle hits the dog who runs away yelping. He ….
- His roommate in the hostel was disturbing everyone's study time by playing loud music. He….

As you go along in the test, you may find similar situations being depicted; read carefully before putting your reaction to the same. The story may have a slight twist, and therefore, be careful!

When you read about situations like the ones I have enumerated, what, and how do you think? Obviously, you would like to help the train passengers, help the child and check on the dog who crossed the street. The solution stares at you in the face. But different people will react differently to the same inputs and your reaction can be unique and very different from your friend. Try it out as an exercise.

How or what you would do is what you need to write, and this will be your unique reaction that comes instantly to your mind. Since everyone comes from varied backgrounds and have different concepts and practical knowledge, morals, and morality, the reactions are different, even though all would like to help a person in distress.

Therefore, this is a test of your common sense, and about how different humans react to everyday situations. The situations may go from being extremely easy at the beginning but may take a little more thinking/doing as the test progresses. At some point during the test, you will begin to feel stressed due to time constraints.

If you cannot think clearly, pause, take a few deep breaths and then get back on track. This can be done while you read through the situation. The other method of course is to tell yourself consciously to 'relax' repeating the word, a few times. This will help relax your mind. Simultaneously, clench and unclench your fist a couple of times.

Do you need to train for the SRT? In my opinion, no training is required as this is a test of your common sense. My advice is that you need not practice answering to the many situations given in SSB books and the internet. What you need to practice, however, is to be able to think fast and then jot down your thoughts in writing in a few words. Therefore, a person with a fair command over the language will be able to give this test with ease.

In some books and classes conducted for SSB, I have been told that you are also trained and coached for responses in the SRT. They will teach you to give positive, calibrated responses and force you to go with this baggage in your mind for the test—this may prove to be counterproductive.

Anyone who is quick on the uptake, has a positive frame of mind and can take bold and correct decisions under pressure is likely to do well in this test.

As soon as you come to the end of this test on your answer sheet, the last test is the Self-Description Test or the SDT.

The Self-Description Test (SDT)

You will be briefed for this test by the psychologist right at the beginning, so please listen to him carefully about what you need to write.

This is nothing but a self-appraisal. How well do you know yourself and how much do you want to reveal to the evaluator? How much do you know of your strengths and weaknesses? Do you remember what I wrote about the SWOT and the essay I asked you to write about yourself? It will be helpful here during this test.

By the time the psychologist comes to checking this part of the test during his evaluation, he would have already formed an image of you in his mind after having gone through your responses. Therefore, this test serves as a confirmatory test for the psychologist.

The SDT is the simplest of this battery of tests and does not (generally!) lead to any stress. You are expected to write about yourself in 15 minutes in the format given. If you have done the homework I had told you about the PIQ tree, this test would be a breeze for you since you wouldn't have to jog your mind about what to write. This is one test that you can prepare for well in advance. But remember, out here too, one needs to be truthful!

The evaluator will, in any case have a fair idea about you after he has gone through what you have written in the preceding tests. As I have told you earlier, we are trained to find out if someone is trying to conceal facts or is writing something that is not true. Therefore, the best way is the 'right' and truthful way. Here is your chance to freely talk about yourself.

You can start this essay with a brief introduction to yourself and of your background.

Thereafter, write about your educational and professional achievements and what you have planned for your future.

After the introduction, you can describe your personality by telling the evaluator about your friends, teachers, parents, and siblings and your relationship with each of them, what you think of them and what they think about you. You also need to write about what you think of yourself and how you see yourself in the future.

You could cover your likes and dislikes as also your strengths and weaknesses in a paragraph. You can also tell the evaluator about the actions or directions that you have taken to get rid of some of your traits that you would like to change. Only a person who is self-aware can write about his weaknesses and how he plans to improve upon his shortcomings.

Some of the common faults that I have observed in this test are:

- Candidates write a lot about unimportant things and spend a lot of time on the introduction. Their essay, therefore, is lopsided and does not convey their real personality.
- Some boys and girls tend to brag a lot about their plus points and dismiss their shortcomings in a couple of sentences. Your essay should be well-rounded and balanced.
- Some candidates write things that do not conform to the briefing for the test as well as what you have written in your PIQ form.
- You need to paraphrase this essay well and not go about writing it haphazardly. You would have prepared for this exercise well, and hopefully will be able to write neatly without any cutting or omissions.

- You can read examples given online on this test and choose a few words that best describe your personality. Use these words only if these **really** relate to you. Ensure that you understand the meaning of the words you use to describe yourself. This will improve the readability of your essay.

This test done, you can enjoy a well-deserved rest before the other tests start the next day. Do not get demoralised if you think the test hasn't gone well. Instead, look forward for the GTO and the individual interview planned for you, next.

Group Testing

The group dynamic can bring synergy, or tear things apart.
–Margaret Bau

If I must go back in time to my tests at the Services Selection Board, and someone asks me which test was the most enjoyable, I would, without doubt, zero in on the Group Testing Segment of the five-day process. I remember clearly what all happened through this series; even today, I wonder how I passed this test at the SSB!

Back then, one had to be cleared by all three assessors to pass, unlike today, where, if you are cleared by one assessor, you could still pass if you make it to the minimum required grade/marks.

I was lean, thin, all of forty-five kg or so, barely fifteen and a half, shy and under-confident, and suffered from stage fright. In my group there were six-footer guys, well-matured, strong, and confident, and I felt that I would be outdone by these hunks in this mostly 'physical' group test. As I look back, and having been an assessor myself, I now realise how wrong I was in my own self-assessment at that time!

Many wannabes are paranoid about the GTO test and attend various training centres and academies to learn techniques to pass this test. This is not required, but it would be good to know what happens in this test and understand the purpose of this test and how you can prepare for this assessment in the correct manner.

The technique uses a set of indoor and outdoor tasks that check your verbal and written expressions, as well as your mental and physical abilities while working in a group.

You must have been part of a group so many times, whether as part of a group performing on stage, or as part of a football team or group doing certain experiments in the laboratory. When one is part of a group, your persona and behaviour undergoes change. It is said that group activities bring out the best in a person, as is amply seen in the sports field where the spirit of competition and the will to win makes members of the group excel and co-operate to accomplish group goals.

You can get a diverse set of people together, (even if they have never met) and give them a task. This group will transform into a team now. While some members will plan and coordinate, some will do the physical part of the work, while others will do something else to make sure that the group's goal is achieved. In every group, there will also be people who will talk more and work less, while some will just remain silent spectators. All kinds of people make up this world and groups, too; but even though some will become leaders, some workers, and some onlookers, all will agree that the group will act like a team, right?

That is exactly what the GTO is trying to assess and watches what role you play in the group activities. This series of tests at the SSB is the only time you are in direct contact with the assessor for a prolonged period. The interview is more formal, with the interviewer interacting with you, one-on-one for about forty-five minutes or so.

The first word of caution that I must give you here is that you are doing this test for yourself; there is no competition with your fellow mates, and therefore, there is no requirement to plan your actions just to impress the evaluator, just like as in the psych test. Suffice it to say that you must just be part of this team and do what you have to, even if the GTO or anyone else is not overseeing what is happening or what you are doing. As I have reiterated many times here, let the assessor do his job, while you do yours. That is the best mantra.

When is this group formed? If you remember, it was on the day you got screened and were allotted fresh chest numbers and made to stay in one room together. That was the first step in making this group into a team. You would have interacted with your group in your leisure time and got 'connected' with each member. The team will now be taken through a series of tests where the bonding and bonhomie will only get stronger.

In the armed forces especially, one needs to operate as a team to win over the enemy. People may be excellent individuals and professionals, but may not be good team players and this is extremely detrimental to group goals. The armed forces would rather have average professionals who are good group and team players to work with at all jobs.

At the SSB, one of the most important factors that assessors look for in a personality is the individual's capacity and capability to work in a group. Anyone who gives the indication of being a loner and an individualist is weaned out by the assessor, however good he may perform. A person who is a loner and displays poor social skills does not make a good friend or an effective team player; therefore, he or she will not make a good leader.

In the armed forces, from the day you don the uniform, you will be in-charge of men who look up to you as a demi-god and are even willing to face the bullet for you; therefore, I reiterate that the armed forces is always looking for men and women who possess a high level of such skills.

To summarise, the GTO is looking for:
- A person who is an effective and contributing member of a group.
- The group's ability to be cohesive in task achievement. This requires contributions of all group members (and, therefore, yours too).
- The person(s) ability in the group to deal with stress at work, and to win over obstacles to achieve group goals.

The GTO tests

The GTO will take you through nine tests in three phases. Phase-1 is the 'Basic series' which include:
- Group Discussion (GD) (Indoor)
- Group Planning Exercise (GPE) (Indoor)
- Progressive Group Task (PGT) (Outdoor)
- Group Obstacle Race (GOR) (Outdoor)

These tests help the GTO to evaluate the candidate in a leaderless group and this forms the GTO's first impression.

Phase 2 is the 'Confirmatory series' of tests which include:
- Half Group Task (HGT) (Outdoor)
- Individual Obstacles (IO) (Outdoor)
- Lecturette (Indoor)
- Command Task (CT) (Outdoor)

In this phase, the assessor has a closer look at each candidate and verifies his findings that he made in the basic series of tests.

Phase-3 test has just one component:
The Final Group Task or the FGT.
In this phase, the group is re-integrated and the assessor now re-confirms some of the personality traits in borderline individuals or checks on some individuals on whom he has a doubt or query.

The three phases of these tests are spread over two days, and as I said earlier, are quite enjoyable. Some of the friendships and bonding that develop during this phase will lead to life-long relationships.

The entire GTO series of tests are done in PT dress or tracksuits. Ensure that you have well-fitting shoes, a good pair of socks as well as a clean outfit for the test. If I was to go for the SSB again, I would carry an extra pair of shorts and tee-shirt for the tests just to be on the safe side.

★★★

> It's time now to discuss each of the GTO tasks.

A Series of Tests

A good discussion increases the dimensions of everyone who takes part.
—**Margaret Mead**

Test – 1 Group Discussion

You have already been through a group discussion in your Phase-1 screening that involved a discussion on the picture that you saw briefly on the screen. This test is slightly different in the sense that the other two assessors are missing and there is no imaginary story to be discussed. The GTO will give you two topics for discussion. The first one is easy—and is a topic of your choice which the group chooses from a list with the GTO. The second one is slightly difficult. The GTO decides on the topic.

Both discussions go on for about fifteen to twenty minutes each, with free and fair debate without interjections from the GTO. Sometimes, the GTO may intervene to channelise your thoughts and encourage some of the 'quiet' members to speak.

What is being seen here is your depth of knowledge, your spoken and convincing skills, confidence, poise, your ability to think clearly and to put across your point of view. Often, some candidates just speak for the sake of speaking, and waste everyone's time.

Keep the following points in mind during this GD:
- Form up and firm up your thoughts once the topic is decided.
- Do not talk unnecessarily; come to the point, and express an opinion.
- Give adequate examples from your life or about what you have read on the topic.
- Listening is as important as speaking. When the others are talking, listen and think what you would like to comment on. Interject at an opportune moment to voice your agreement or disagreement.
- Respect the others' points of view. Only your views cannot be correct or be accepted. Hence, do not be overbearing or have a dissenting tone or try and put down someone.
- Body language is important. Do not get over-excited and jump about or gesticulate unnecessarily to make a point. Maintain a fair degree of restraint. Smile and keep things relaxed. Eye contact is important and so is your tone and tenor.
- Be truthful, straightforward, and energetic in the group. It should not be an outward show but must come from within.
- Use simple and easy-to-use language. Big bombastic words will be counterproductive.
- If the discussion is veering off the main topic, try and get it back on track.
- It is not about how much or how many times you spoke which is important; it is **what** you spoke or the meat of the matter that is vital.

What is it that one can do to train for group discussions? Even in the outside world, GDs are carried out for job interviews. To train yourself, you can:

- Read extensively on current topics. This is most important and will lead to confidence in what you speak. The internet is a good source for remaining abreast of what is happening in the world.
- Practice discussions with your friends.
- Learn the art of speaking less and conveying more.
- Learn to remain calm in discussions.
- Learn to be a good listener.
- Being 'yourself' is the secret to success.
- You can practice speaking along with your friends and manage your tone, speed of delivery, tone and tenor, and other aspects of public speaking.

Test - 2: The Group Planning Exercise

This is one very interesting indoor exercise I encountered at the SSB. In this exercise, every member of the group is made to plan, both individually and as the leader of the group. The task is to find solutions to a set of problems given out in a story which is explained on a model. The plan is to be written and discussed to arrive at a final, consensus solution or group plan.

The GTO will first introduce to you the test, then tell you what needs to be done. Listen carefully.

Either with the help of a scale model or of a chart, the GTO will narrate a story from a card that will be available to each group member as well. He will explain the story, going through it twice before he asks the candidates to read it individually to understand it better with the help of the model.

The story line could be something like this:

You are a group of four or five boys. You are on a picnic to a jungle where you meet an old man who tells you that there has been a robbery in the village close by and the robbers were also overheard speaking about stopping a local train which passes through the area in the evening and robbing the passengers. They have also taken a few village boys as hostage and are hiding somewhere in the jungle as of now. A local villager on his bullock cart has had a minor accident and needs some medical attention....

The story will go on like this. Very much like a suspense novel or movie! After he finishes the narration, he will brief you on the ground rules which may go something like this: No one is to operate alone and all must move in groups of at least two. You are allowed to hitch a lift, wherein the time taken to reach the site of the accident spot is ....hours and the time taken to reach the proposed robbery site is .....hours and the road accident is so many miles away from your position and other such details like where the police station is located, where is the nearest hospital etc.

After the narration, you will be told what actions are needed—in this case, you need to warn the railway station master in time to stop the train at the station so that the robbery does not take place, inform the police of the location of the robbers and also take care of the injured bullock cart driver etc.

You will be asked to write the solution to the entire problem giving out the complete plan, which will be followed by a discussion. Remember, you are to find a **solution** as the **leader** of the group and take your ideas to the discussion.

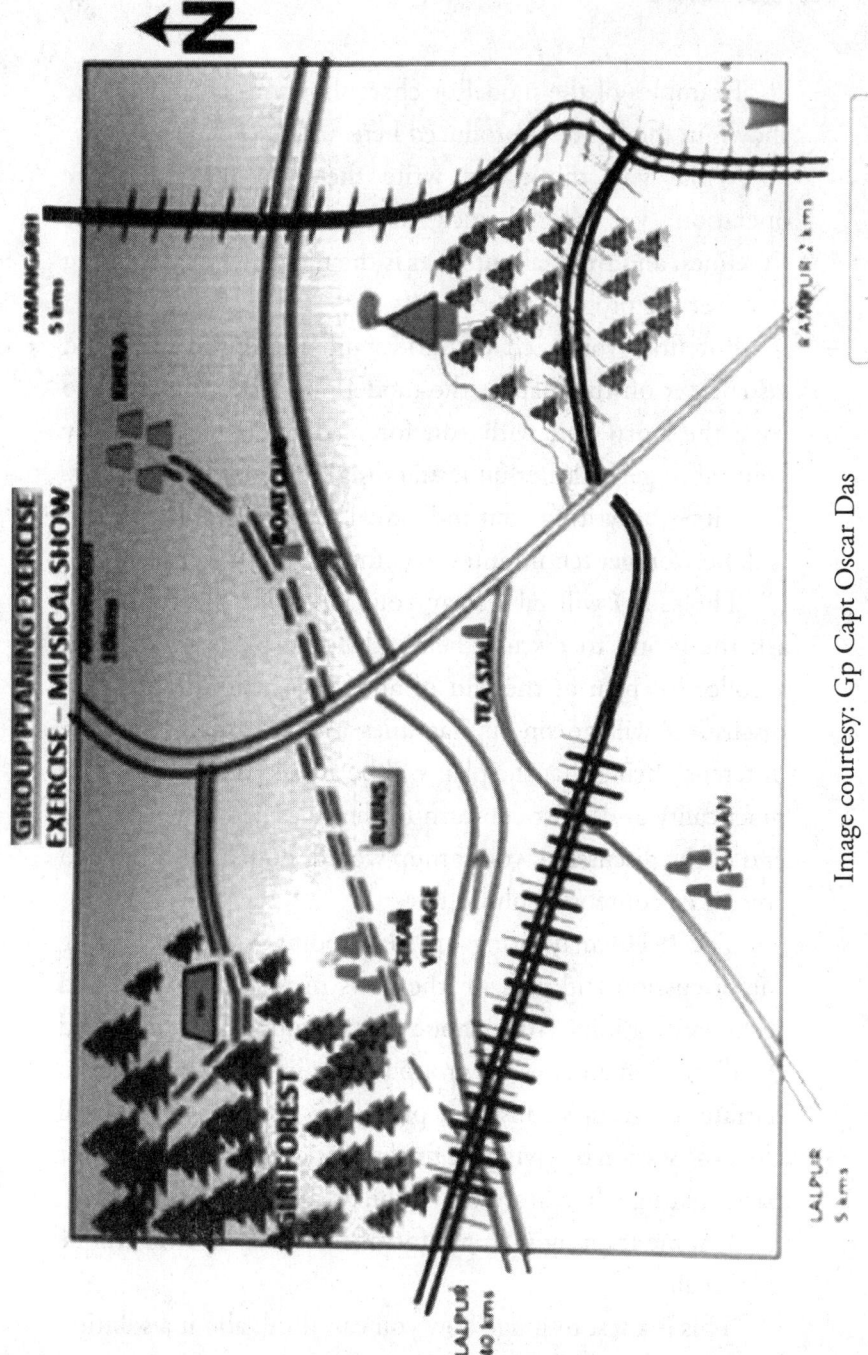

Image courtesy: Gp Capt Oscar Das

Examples of the model or chart shown to candidates are shown in the figures reproduced here.

While you think and write the plan for the entire operation, you should stick to the rules, adhere to the timelines, and think about what is the most practical solution to the entire problem.

But first, you need to understand the entire story and visualise it on the map or the model provided. You will also have the story card with you for reading it once again by yourself to get a clearer understanding for about five minutes. The time for writing your individual solution starts after this is done. You get ten minutes to complete this assignment.

The GTO will take away your solutions sheet and will ask the group to discuss their individual plans to arrive at a collective plan at the end of about twenty minutes. This discussion will go on similar lines as the earlier GDs, the difference being that the plan will be argued out, checked for practicality and must conform to the rules laid down. At the end of the discussion, your group would, hopefully, be able to come to a consensus solution.

The GTO may bring up some points or issues during the discussion and pick on the flaws in the group plan and seek clarifications. After about twenty minutes, he will end the discussion and ask the group to nominate one member to narrate the group's consensus plan. This done, the GTO will close the session by giving his final remarks and thanking all for participating wholeheartedly in the planning and discussion.

Is some training required for this test? My answer will be 'No' again!

This is a test to judge how you can think about a solution to a slightly complex problem, how you are able to understand the larger picture and plan something workable, which when integrated, is a solution to the entire problem. This is a test of your mental skills and since you have made it this far, I do not see any reason why you will not be able to do this exercise with ease. Keep your wits about you, keep calm and think clearly and practically when you attempt this test.

To summarise the GPE:
- Read and understand the story.
- Identify the number of problems that need to be solved.
- What is the priority of each of the activities that need to be done (For example, saving a life will be most important).
- Keep a track of the timelines when you plan.
- What are the resources—both human and material that are available to you? How do you plan to utilise these, with best results?
- Think practically; how can the tasks be achieved realistically?
- Keep a look out for the red-herring. Unimportant tasks need not be given much importance.
- Always keep the **Aim** in mind and then decide on the objectives and end results that you must achieve. This is important as one often tends to drift away when the aim is not kept in mind.
- Write the solution as if you are the leader who is executing and coordinating the entire task.

After the GPE, it will be now time for a well-deserved tea break, post which the GTO will take all candidates to the group testing area where you will see the next part of your GTO tasks, waiting for you. These are usually outdoor activities.

But before we move out to the outdoor arena, it would be appropriate for me to explain the tasks in the Progressive Group Task (PGT), Half Group Task (HGT) and the Command Task (CT) sections.

The outdoor tasks

You must have played or watched children playing *stapu* or hopscotch as it is formally called. There are rules one has to follow to get across the grid drawn on the ground. What you will undergo in these three outdoor tests is somewhat similar.

On the ground, you will see some structures of wood and metal, some close to the ground, some at a height, and some zig-zags painted in various colour codes. On the ground, a line in white painted bricks, depicts the start and a similar line across the obstacle will depict the finish line. Between these two lines is the 'play' or game area where all the rules described and explained by the GTO have to be followed.

The purpose of the wooden structures marked in different colours will be explained to you and you will be told which area of the structure can be used, stepped on, or not used at all. The GTO will also brief you about certain areas which are out of bounds and cannot be used or even touched by the 'helping material.' (This term will be discussed in the next paragraph). There could be a few areas on the structures where only one person is permitted at a time and some areas where 'helping material' is not allowed and things like that.

The aim of the game is to take the entire team across the obstacle(s) along with a 'critical load,' generally a heavy tin filled with sand. 'Helping material' is given to you, such as a *balli* (a bamboo pole), one *phatta* (plank) and a rope. These can be used singularly or in combination to help you go across the obstacle. You could make makeshift bridges, or use them in any other way to get across the obstacle grid.

You must understand that this is a game of the brain rather than brawn. We do not want to see dangerous, gymnastic or acrobatic moves where you put yourself in danger, nor do we want to evaluate your athletic prowess, or see your physical strength! All the obstacles have multiple simple solutions which require some 'out of the box thinking.' In short, it makes you use your practical intelligence.

My advice to you, therefore, is to use your common sense and find a practical 'workable' solution to the problems. You will realise that it may not be a straightforward solution where you just put a plank and walk across. It will force you to be innovative.

During my days as an assessor, I have seen many candidates who act without thinking, making audacious and foolish plans which just cannot work. This happens either because you are overwhelmed by the situation and cannot think clearly, or because you want to impress the GTO! Such situations are not worth getting into.

During these tests, the assessor will observe you closely as you go about the tasks. Some of you will argue out your ideas, some will be willing to help in the overall aim while some will prefer to remain mute onlookers. What you need to do is to try out ideas, speak to each other, respect others' plans and views and, also ask others to outline their solutions. It is a collective effort and if someone tries to show that he or she alone can manage the game or lead the team to success, they will be sadly mistaken!

Test - 3: Progressive Group Task

The Progressive Group Task is first on the list. This is the longest and the most stressful.

Forty-five minutes is allotted to get across four sets of obstacles. After briefing you in detail, the GTO will withdraw and watch from a distance. He will sit in a chair, under a shade, and make his notes and observations on each of the candidates. As usual, it is best not to bother about him; instead, look at the task in hand.

The GTO will get impressed by what you *say* and *do* rather than what you want to try and show him! I have seen candidates who keep looking at the GTO trying hard to attract his attention; in doing that, they lose sight of what needs to be done. It is best to disregard the GTO. Listen to him only when he speaks to the group!

In his briefing, the GTO explains the different rules for the game. There are group rules, distance rules, rules for the 'helping material' and the load which need to be followed in spirit. If you break a rule, you are supposed to go back to the start line and commence all over again. For example, if you lose your balance and touch the ground which is out of bounds, you need to get back to the start line. You need not see if the GTO has seen the rule being broken, just go by the instructions given in the beginning. That is a mark of your integrity, isn't it?

The GTO may, if he wishes, allow you to carry on from the point where the rule was broken to save time. He may also ask some general questions on why a particular action is being done or may also give a hint about how to go about the task!

As soon as the test starts, the group is on its own and can commence planning and execution. Often, in these tests I have noticed trained candidates trying to use their previous knowledge or templates that they had seen before during their 'training' and apply that knowledge here. It may not always work.

No set of obstacles is the same anywhere. They require on-the-spot understanding, planning and execution. Do not keep trying something that defies the laws of physics and gravity. Look for workable solutions and this can be done only if you are calm, collected, and willing to use your brains.

Remember, there is no nominated leader in the group. It is the group's collective responsibility to come up with solutions and not the duty of just a single or a few group members. Also remember, the weakest link in the group has to be catered for and keep each individual's capacity and capability in mind when plans are made. A lot of groups that I have observed, do not cater to getting the last man across, which defeats the final aim of the exercise. Also, some groups tend to ignore the 'critical load' which also must be taken across the finish line. Keep this in mind in your planning.

The test begins and a lot of ideas are discussed and tried out. Time seems to be at a premium, as always, and stress due to panic can affect some participants.

The first obstacle is generally easy and the degree of difficulty increases thereafter. In my years at the SSB, I have seen good groups getting to the fourth obstacle in the allotted time, while a mediocre or low-level group barely manages to get across one or two obstacles with their combined efforts and some efforts of the GTO!

Remember, it is how you attempt and how you apply yourself that matters!

At the end of this test, it will be time for the most enjoyable and noisy Group Obstacle Race (GOR) or the Snake Race as it is popularly called.

Test - 4: The Group Obstacle Race (GOR)

All the groups gather at the beginning of a linear set of simple obstacles made of wooden beams and poles. Every group must get across each of these obstacles while competing with the other groups, carrying an unwieldly long and heavy 'snake' across these set of obstacles.

The snake is generally a thick rope with jute bags tied around it to make it bulky and heavy. It is usually eight to ten feet in length, and the entire group must carry the snake across the obstacles without letting it touch the ground. The rules of the game are similar. If the snake touches the ground, the group falls back to the previous obstacle and continues with the race. All members must cross the obstacles in the manner demonstrated before the race begins.

This race happens with a lot of cheering and war cries and becomes quite a melee, but that helps in banishing the stress built up during the previous tasks. The snake race is, therefore, thoroughly enjoyable and lots of fun. It tends to get sweaty and muddy during this race, and it is fun to see candidates with their clothes dirty, their faces red and dishevelled as they gasp for breath at the finish line with a sense of accomplishment on their faces!

In this test too, a similar set of rules like the PGT apply. The requirement is to cross over the obstacles with the snake in hand together as a group. You are allowed to help each other, be active participants and show how much *josh* you have. But let not this *josh* lead to lessening of your *hosh* or awareness, which is equally important.

At the end of the basic series of tests, the GTO will check if you all are okay and if you enjoyed the group tasks of day one. He will also tell you what will happen in part two of the

GTO series, to be held the next day. You now get back to your rooms for a well-earned rest.

Some SSBs are forced to resort to a single day test for the GTO series due to administrative constraints. In such a case, the second set of tests will generally be carried out post-lunch. This, however, is an exception rather than a rule.

You will be all bubbly and happy when you leave the GTO grounds and the discussions will continue for a long time through the day. You will feel the bonhomie, care, respect and understanding that has been generated among the group members, just in a few hours of working together. You all will now look forward to what's coming next in the second series of tests planned for the next day.

I have been told by many candidates that the so-called 'trained' candidates within the group try and make subgroups for the Command task, and tell you what topics to study for the lecturette; in short, they take it upon themselves to 'brief' everyone in detail as if they are the GTOs themselves!

Before the Command task, some over-enthusiastic, 'poorly trained' candidates pre-decide on the helpers they will call for their command tasks. This is to negate the advantage that will occur if one of the more popular candidates is called by many. It is wrongly understood by some of the candidates that the greater number of times a particular person is called for help, the better are his or her chances of passing the SSB.

Prior planning is not required since the command tasks for everyone is different. Leave it to the GTO to ensure that each of you get a chance at being a helper. So, if people in your group try to pre-plan this, dissuade them from doing so. As you go through the next set of tests, the next day, you will realise that prior planning does not work at all!

Let us now examine the confirmatory series of tests, one by one.

Day 2 Tests: GTO

The day 2 tests begin at the GTO grounds, itself, after you have had your breakfast. Please make sure that you are well-rested and relaxed for this round. The first test is the Half Group task or the HGT.

Test - 5: The Half Group Task (HGT)

The test is like the PGT the previous day. This time, however, the group is split into two and just a single set of obstacles awaits the first half of the group at the ground, while the other half awaits their turn in the waiting room.

There would have been some among you who would not have been able to show your true self or may not have 'opened up' while working in a larger group. The smaller size of the group will allow such individuals to perform better. The GTO, on the other hand, has a fewer number of candidates to study and can observe each of them more minutely.

As you go through the HGT, you will realise that you would have already learnt a thing or two of how to get across obstacles using the helping material in the PGT. This test is essentially a repeat of the same test, but on a different set of obstacles. The only difference is that you will be more confident this time!

The time allotted for this test is about 15 to 20 minutes and it has similar rules to be followed. Once this test is over, the second group is called to the ground and they go through it as well.

After this test, participants must now show the GTO how well they speak on a selected topic in front of a small audience during the Lecturette to be held in a specified area of the GT ground.

Test - 6 The Lecturette

The lecturette is a three-minute extempore talk on varied and commonly discussed topics of general interest. You will stand in order of your chest numbers in a semi-circle and the GTO will brief you on the rules.

He will have three to four topics written down on small chits of paper placed in a basket. From the choice of the topics available on your chit of paper that you will pick up, you can choose any one. You will get three minutes to stand in a corner to prepare for this and, thereafter, you will be called to speak to the group. The GTO rings a warning bell at two minutes and thirty seconds to help you to wind up your talk. If you exceed the time allotted, the GTO may bring about an abrupt end to your talk.

Meanwhile, the next candidate in line would have already collected his chit and gone to a corner to prepare for his talk while the first person is speaking. Even if the previous person finishes his talk early, everyone gets their stipulated three minutes to prepare for the talk.

The topics could range from Women in the Armed Forces; The internet of things; CTBT; War in Ukraine; World Cup Cricket; Make in India; Aadhar Revolution; Sports in India; Crisis in Gaza; The United Nations and many other similar topics. If you have been reading the newspapers and have kept yourself abreast of what is happening in the world, this lecturette will be easy for you.

How does one train for such talks? Most importantly, if you have the knowledge, then you will have the confidence to speak among your peers. So, please commence reading newspapers and keep yourself updated on current affairs.

If I were to prepare myself for short talks, I would do the following:
- Read up about how a semi-formal extempore talk is to be given. Essentially, the talk must have an introduction, a middle body (meat of the matter) and a conclusion that may or may not have your own recommendations depending on the topic. Since you have just three minutes (try timing yourself out to speak for that time—it would seem like three hours!) in which to give out everything, plan on about thirty seconds of introduction, about two minutes of the middle body and the last thirty seconds to conclude what you have said.
- More important is to learn how to gather your thoughts on the topic in the three minutes of preparation time that you will get before you speak. There is no pen and paper provided, so the points must be brought out from memory. This can only happen with lots of practice. I suggest that you gather like-minded friends two or three times a week to practice for this test.
- Another advise that I give my students is to maintain a diary or notebook where you keep writing small essays on various topics of current interest and practice speaking on these when you get the time. If you start early, you would have enough topics under your belt by the time you go in for your SSB. Magazines on current topics like the *Competition Success Review, India Today, Frontline* etc., are a good source for preparation.

Here are some more tips while attempting this task at the SSB:
- Stand smartly in front of your friends. Remember that they too are going through the same test and are as anxious as you are.
- The group in front of you are as knowledgeable or ignorant as you are. There are no questions or comments at the end of your talk, so do not worry about this.
- Use simple and easy-to-understand language.
- Speak loudly and clearly so that all your friends can hear you. Avoid addressing the GTO or looking at him. Your tone and modulation say a lot about your confidence.
- Maintain a pleasant disposition. Smile, maintain eye contact with everyone and avoid excessive gesticulation. Best would be to stand with your hands behind your back if possible.
- It would be good to introduce the topic with a personal example. It will draw everyone's attention and you will feel confident right from the beginning. If you add a relevant fact, figure or a funny episode about the topic, you will be able to sustain the audience's attention throughout.

The following diagram will give you a fair idea of how to give an extempore talk.

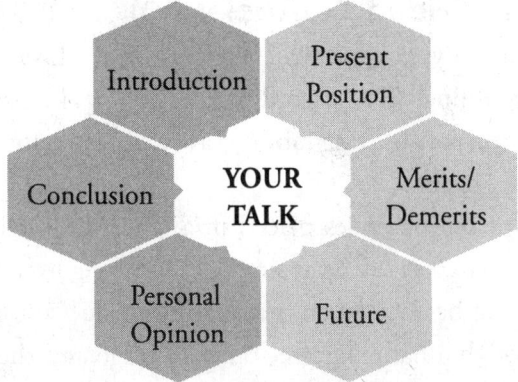

I remember very clearly what happened to me in my SSB during this exercise. It turned out to be a complete disaster! The topic I got to speak on was 'Religion,' about which I really knew nothing about in those days. And there weren't multiple choices of topics as you get to choose from now. That tensed me up, and in the three minutes I got to prepare, I could only think of a few lines to speak. Added to that was my stage fright which turned me into jelly knees in front of my friends. I started with a few sentences, then went into a long pause, drawing a blank! With all those eyes fixed on me, I was embarrassed and apologised to everyone that I did not have anything more to say on the topic since I had almost no knowledge of the same.

I did, however, get selected at the SSB! In hind sight, I think the GTO was happy that I was genuine and truthful and, therefore, passed me!

But come to think of it, it is your *overall performance* in the whole series of tests that is important. One odd test that does not go well should not demoralise you or affect your performance.

The Individual Obstacles are the next in line once you finish with the extempore talks.

Test - 7 Individual Obstacles (IO)

This is the only exercise which checks you a little for your physical stamina. But according to me, it is also a test of your decision-making ability as well as planning and organising prowess.

A set of ten obstacles placed in a circle are used for this test. The obstacles may be as simple as jumping over a rope or walking on a balance beam, graduating to difficult ones like going through a hanging tyre, Burma bridge and the famous

Tarzan leap as most candidates love to call it. Each of these are placed randomly and are numbered according to their degree of difficulty from 1 to 10. The number on the obstacles is also the mark that you will get for clearing it.

The GTO will brief you for the exercise and take you to each of the obstacles explaining how it is to be done. Having ensured that there are no questions or doubts, the whole group will wait in the resting area and await their turn.

You are to finish the ten obstacles in three minutes. If you manage to do all, you can even repeat a few in the time left to gain extra marks. The GTO leaves it to you to decide which obstacles to take on first and the order in which you would like to do them. Similar rules as for the other outdoor test are applicable here, too. If you break the rule, the obstacle needs to be repeated. It all depends on you and on which obstacle you want to attempt first. There is no correct way prescribed.

The exercise begins on a call from the GTO who times you out on a stop-watch. At two minutes and thirty seconds, he blows the whistle. This is also an indication to the next person to get ready to start.

Some important points to keep in mind for this exercise are:
- Ensure that you have well-fitting shoes and clothes for the exercise.
- Make a plan and stick to it as far as possible.
- Avoid wasting time or doing things haphazardly.
- Waste minimum time between obstacles. Have a sense of urgency and run from one obstacle to the other.
- If you break the rules, go back to the start line of that obstacle. A lot of candidates try and look at the GTO to ask him if they can carry on.

- Do not bother about the GTO or onlookers.
- Do not be foolhardy and end up injuring yourself.
- If there is an obstacle which you cannot get over, try again but do not waste attempts and time if you feel that it is not possible for you to do it. If you have not done one or more obstacles, there is no point in repeating other obstacles since it will not fetch you additional marks.

If you are keen to get hands-on training for this part of the test, you could go to any armed forces or NCC unit in your town or city and request the officials there to use the obstacle course where similar structures are available. I am sure if you approach the authorities and tell them your intention, they will be willing to help you.

Let us now go to another interesting test, the Command Task which is next in line.

Test - 8 The Command Task (CT)

So far, all the tasks that you did were leaderless tasks. The command task is the only one which will allow you to be a leader of the group. You will be called the 'commander' for this task and will be allowed to call for two to three helpers from your group. (Remember what I had said about pre-planning these?)

While the rest of the group is sitting inside the waiting area, you will be welcomed at the task area by the GTO where he will engage you in small talk and ask you perhaps, about your background, schooling and how your stay at the SSB has been. Answer his questions confidently and await his briefing.

He will introduce the task to you much in the same manner as he did the earlier ones. After he confirms that you have no doubts about the task, he will ask you to nominate any of your group members as helpers for the task. Generally, two helpers are enough for any of the command tasks which need to be completed in about 10-15 minutes. By the time the helpers arrive, you should have planned on how you are going to get across the obstacle.

Your time starts as soon as your helpers arrive; the task commences from that point. Explain the task to your team and tell them what you plan to do. Assign work to your team members. This time around, the helpers will do as you tell them. The plan is yours and the way you utilise the help available to you is also entirely up to you. Similar rules for other exercises apply here as well.

This exercise is actually simpler than the ones you have gone through, till now. You need to keep your wits about you and plan with a clear mind. Please treat the helpers with respect and give clear and concise orders which they can understand and obey. You are not permitted to ask your helpers for suggestions. This is a team exercise and all of you need to get across with the load. Many times, commanders only pass orders and stand away from obstacles. That is not what good commanders do. They lead from the front, take control and give a helping hand in the task, as well.

It is team effort even though you are the leader. As captain of any team, you'd try and put in more effort to motivate your team, won't you? The members of the team will follow you better and put in their best efforts if you lead them this way.

When you join the armed forces, you will be in command of men and material from day one onwards, and this responsibility increases as you rise in service. This command task is just the beginning of your journey!

Remember what I told you about fixing the helpers beforehand? Ask for only those people whom you feel will be best suited for the job. You may require a light person for a particular job or a tall one for another. Do not indulge in 'match fixing' and get into a fix!

As you wait in the room for your turn, do not ask the candidates who have finished their task for a quick brief. That's because the tasks for each one in the group may be different, and it may lead to confusion!

The command task over, it will now be time for the entire group to come together one final time for the Final Group Task.

Test - 9 The Final Group Task (FGT)

This is the task in which the GTO will have one final look at each of you while doing a single task. If he has had any doubts about his assessment about a particular candidate, he will take a relook now. Therefore, do not take this test lightly since it maybe you who is under his lens! I have seen some borderline candidates pass due to their performance in this test. I am saying this because I have heard that candidates who come after training tell their friends that this test is just 'time pass,' since the GTO has already made up his mind about who is going to pass. This, I assure you, is not a correct assessment.

This test is like the PGT but with a single obstacle set which is generally an easy one. The members of the group are now good friends and understand each other much better; and by now, all are conversant with the rules of the game. Moreover, you are already well-versed with the process and you would have put your inhibitions behind you; this test will be simple and you will cross over to the other side without a problem.

The GTO, as usual, introduces the test to you all and then leaves you to solve the puzzle in front of you. This is another 15 to 20 minute exercise, and the last one in the series for the GTO.

As soon as you are done with the test, the GTO will speak to you for a few minutes. He will also ask you some general questions about the test series and check if you all are feeling good and charged up after the experience.

He will wish you well for the rest of the tests and bid you goodbye. When he does that, you are actually going to feel sad that the GTO series of tests are over. The assessor will now go through his notes and calculate the final marks and results, based across all the nine tests.

When you walk back to your rooms after this is done, you will start missing the last two days of intense activity and fun! The GTO series, in my view, is the most enjoyable and exciting for all participants. You may not realise it, but you are a changed personality at the end of these tests. You start understanding the importance of team-work, cooperation, being kind, respecting other's views, and realising the value of pursuing your goals relentlessly to achieve what is desired.

It is now time for the chapter on the interview and the techniques you need to know. A few from your group may have had their interviews earlier, followed by the GTO series or vice versa depending on how the plan was made.

The Interview: One on One

One important key to success is self-confidence. An important key to self-confidence is preparation.
—Arthur Ashe

What is an interview? Have you been through one?

The dictionary describes it thus: *An interview is a conversation between two or more people where questions are asked to the interviewee; the answers given are analysed to see if the interviewee is fit for the job.* It is qualitative research and can be done in many ways, directly or indirectly. Online surveys, questionnaires, video and telephonic conversations could also form part of an interview.

I suppose all of us would have gone through an interview to get to a school, to get selected for a competition to represent your school or college or simply been spoken to formally by your teacher to counsel you. All these can be called interviews.

What is the purpose of an interview and when does the requirement arise? The answer is simple—one can have an interview when we have more than the required applicants for a job. It is a question of high supply Vs. low demand and in such a situation, there is a need to screen and weed out some of the candidates, so that we are able to choose the best from among the many candidates who have applied for the post. Thereafter, further shortlisting of candidates is done based on their competence and performance, and a final merit list allows the employer to call the chosen candidates to join the organisation in the order of their rank.

The Phase 1 testing or the Day-1 procedure of screening at the SSB is also a type of interview. Interviews can be done with many interviewers or one can have a panel interview. Interviews can be done over a formal lunch or dinner, or could go into many rounds (technical, HR etc.,).

Let us now check out the personal interview carried out at the SSB. How does one prepare for it? The interview is a mix of both the structured and unstructured, and training academies may prepare you for the structured part, but cannot predict what kind of questions you are going to be asked in the other part!

The PIQ tree which I had asked you to make in the earlier chapters will now come in handy as you do your preparation for the interview. I would recommend that you begin preparation for the interview the moment you start preparing for the armed forces. The basic 'to do' list of reading, writing, speaking, being inquisitive, having a hobby etc., is all part of the preparation for the interview. The more knowledgeable you are, the more confident you will be to answer the questions at the interview.

The structured questions at the interview

The basic 'structured' part of the interview at the SSB is in four parts.

The first part deals with your basic information—your education, marks, career options, friends, teachers, games, and participation in sports, extra co-curricular activities or anything related to your education, school and college life.

The second set of questions relate to your family background and the interviewer could ask about your parents, guardians, siblings, about your life at home and about your relationship with your immediate family.

The third set of questions are on your spare time activities, your hobbies, and other interests, about how you keep abreast of what is happening in the world (current affairs), your reading habits, how you manage your budget etc.

The fourth set of questions are about general awareness, armed forces knowledge, general knowledge and may also include some questions related to finding out your depth of knowledge. This part could be interspersed with the first three.

I have often heard candidates describing such questions as 'rapid fire,' just because these are asked in one go to the candidate. The interviewing officer (IO) marks his observations on the answers that you give at the end of each set. He then starts the unstructured part of the interview. In this part, he could ask you questions on whatever you have replied to him, and this could go on for a while till he is satisfied.

For example, if you have answered that you had a 9.8 GPA in your class 10th, 77 per cent in your 11th and scored 65 per cent in your 12th class, he could ask you the reason why your percentage has gone down; what were the distractions; what subjects should you have done better in and so on. When you answer his questions, the conversation could continue in any direction that the interviewer chooses. Only after he is satisfied, will he move on to the next set of questions which are related to what you have already answered.

After the end of the questions and counter questions of

the first set that is related to your education, the IO will move on to the second set of 'rapid fire' questions about your family. The interview will carry on in this manner.

Many candidates try and learn the answers posed in the structured part of the interview by rote since these are available on the internet. This is not the right approach at all. When I conducted interviews, it was very easy for me to know how well the candidate had trained by the way he would answer. It would take me just a few seconds to know if the candidate was answering from rote memory.

Once, on a visit to an SSB training centre, I observed that the candidates were asked to write their answers to each of the sets of rapid fire questions and mug up the same. They were then asked to reproduce the same in the test conducted at the centre! How wrong can this be!

All the assessors are aware of this fact and they often twist around a question or omit a part during the rapid fire. Candidates who do not listen carefully and answer from rote memory soon come to grief. How can anyone answer a question which is not asked? I would often smile to myself when this would happen during the interviews. And may I add that it happened often enough!

It is not so difficult to remember what the interviewer has asked. Listen carefully and then make a mental note of the questions asked and then try and answer the questions in the sequence that they have been asked. In many an interview, I have come across candidates who suddenly draw a blank after their first answer, trying to remember what was asked. They then ask for the questions to be repeated and this is not a very good thing to do; it reflects a muddled state of mind as well as poor organising skills.

After all, *you* have made the PIQ tree, *you* have carried out a SWOT analysis and *you* know yourself the best. The questions posed are about *you* and you should not find it so difficult to remember what was asked; you just need to listen carefully.

We shall return to some more aspects of the interview a little later in this chapter. First, let us see what needs to be done prior to the interview.

Preparations before the SSB interview

The date of your interview will be posted on the notice board and you will be briefed by the duty officer of the day in the evening briefing. Once you have your slotted time, be ready in the waiting room of the candidates' mess at least thirty minutes prior to the time given.

Keep all your certificates with you neatly in a folder and remove unnecessary documents like extra photographs, duplicate certificates, tickets, and other papers—and that includes photos of family as well as deities.

Dressing sense and personal grooming

First impression are formed within seven seconds of meeting someone for the first time. This is true and I quite agree. As the candidate enters the interview room, we assessors observe him or her from top to bottom and form our first impressions.

How was the dress sense? Were the clothes ironed and clean? Had he shaved? Had she taken pains to look well-groomed? Was the shirt clean and the collar too? Were the candidate's nails clipped and clean? Were there loose threads hanging from the buttons? Was the fellow wearing his tie correctly with his collar button closed? Was she comfortable with her attire? The interviewer can take all this in, in just a few seconds!

How should one dress?

Dress in comfortable and formal clothes. By this, I do not mean that you **have** to wear a coat and tie or a formal suit. Dress in a formal trouser, preferably dark and team it up with a light, matching shirt with a belt, matching shoes, and socks. Brown trousers would mean you wear brown shoes and brown socks to match, isn't it?

Many a time, I have seen candidates wear new clothes or even suits for the interview and they are uncomfortable in them, since they have not worn them ever before. My suggestion is that you wear your dress a few times before at home and then get it ironed and ready. After all, you are attending an interview, not going for a wedding! New shoes could bite, and stiff collars may be irritating to your neck, or the belt may be too tight. So, it is important to be comfortable in the clothes you are wearing. There is no requirement to wear blazers or coats when the weather is too hot. The SSB does not dictate that you wear a tie, but if you must, it should be comfortable and tied well, not hanging loose from your neck.

I have often seen boys and girls wear their school or office blazers with their ties not knotted properly or even with their top buttons open. These give a bad impression, so avoid this.

If I was you, I would wear a simple but matching shirt and trouser, and if it was cold, a sweater to keep myself warm. It is good to be simple, yet smart. Also make sure that when you sit, the trouser or coat does not restrict or cramp your movements.

Have a haircut before you come to the SSB centre, and ensure that you do not have the Bollywood style of sidelocks or anything equally bizarre. Clip your nails, so that you look neat and hygienic. Wear only a mild deodorant or cologne that will disturb neither you or the interviewer. Boys should check their moustache and trim it if necessary. If you wear glasses, ensure that they are clean and well-fitting, so that you do not have to fidget with them during the interview.

A word about socks and shoes. The socks, besides being in sync with your trousers should be fresh, and not have loose elastic threads hanging or holes. Shoe laces should be tied neatly and the shoes, of course, must be polished. Many a time, as the candidate sits down in the chair, his shabby socks and frayed laces create a negative impression. In short, dress in neat, clean, and comfortable clothes. Many candidates go out of their way and go overboard in their efforts to look good, wasting time, energy, and money. This is not required.

Here is a note specially for the young women who attend the SSB interview. All the above holds true. In addition, please do not wear revealing clothes or use unnecessary make up. It is best to be in a basic *churidar-kurta* if you are not comfortable in a western or corporate outfit. Make sure that your hair is well tied and combed; use a hairband so that you do not have to keep adjusting your hair when you interact with the IO. Ensure that your clothes and accompaniments are not flashy and gaudy. A simple earring or bangle is okay, but avoid danglers and fancy wrist bands. And, of course, wear sensible footwear.

No pen, paper or diary is allowed to be carried into the interview chamber, so leave it behind in your room. Avoid carrying anything bulky in your pockets. Please carry a clean and ironed handkerchief in your pocket, lest you need one during the interview.

Some of you may be called for the interview during the

day of the GTO test. In this case, you will be specifically told to be in your PT dress/track suit since there may not be time to change your clothes. But, relax, you will get some time to quickly freshen up before the interview. It may, therefore, be a good idea to get rid of the sweat and grime of the GTO test before you head out for the interview.

That was all for the 'physical' preparation for the interview! There is still a lot that needs to be done before the interview.

Mental preparation

Go through your PIQ form in detail before your interview. At night, go through the PIQ tree—it will help you to answer the many questions that the interviewer will be asking you. Also, ensure that you do go through the newspapers and spend some time reading up on current affairs in the evenings when you get time. Go through the diary or Gen-book that I asked you to maintain and brush up on your knowledge of the armed forces. You will realise that a fair amount of preparation for the interview is done at the SSB too.

Avoid asking candidates who have already had their interviews before you about what all was asked. Every interview is handled differently and done by different IOs, who employ different techniques to get to know you. So, avoid talking to your friends who have finished their interviews. You will end up more confused and that will make you tense.

Stress is inevitable in any interview, besides being a part of our daily lives. You need to know what to do when stressed and I have discussed that in the earlier part of this book. Stress can be self-generated or be triggered externally, such as that generated by the interviewer. It can lead to lowering of your thinking mechanism, or even cause a complete shutdown as confusion prevails. I have witnessed this during many an interview.

The last few minutes as you wait outside to be called in to the interview room are the most stressful. I would suggest that you close your eyes, meditate and do some deep breathing which will automatically lower your stress levels. Think that you are going to meet your father's friend or uncle or your teacher to have a heart-to-heart talk.

Like all of us, I, too have faced many a stressful situation in my life. When I get into such a situation, I have always recited a mantra and said 'relax-relax-relax,' over and over again in my mind. One could also think of positive things and good times to bring down stress levels. Simple clenching and unclenching your palms and some focused, deep breathing are some of the other known techniques that are suggested by stress pundits. Choose the one that suits you best.

Know the stressors and the symptoms of stress, which could include tingling sensations in your hands and legs, twitching and frothing lips, knots in your stomach, sweaty hands, shaky legs and the like. Stress will also show on your face and will be immediately noticed by your interviewer who is adept at interpreting body language.

The butterflies in your stomach will soon vanish as you are welcomed into the interview room by the IO. In a few minutes, you will be relaxed and talking freely. Let us try to recreate what will happen after you enter the room.

The interview process

You are now face to face with the IO and in the next 45 minutes or so, you would be through with this major test of the SSB.

Wish the IO a pleasant 'Good Morning' and if he offers you his hand, a firm and not a hurtful handshake is good enough. He will ask you to settle down in the chair positioned just for you. Once the initial greetings are done, and you are settled, he will ask you some basic ice-breaking questions.

The IO, before you have been called in, has already gone through your PIQ form in detail along with the certificates that are in your folder. Some of the IOs I have known (and that includes me) have already googled details about your school, the place you come from, your presence and activities on social media and so on. Therefore, he already has a fair amount of knowledge about you and he would have firmed up on some questions that he plans to ask you.

Breaking ice is nothing but certain pleasantries exchanged between two people who are meeting for the first time. This is done to make you comfortable by asking you some basic questions, something like what would happen if you meet a co-passenger on a plane or train and commence talking to him. Or even like when one meets an acquaintance after many years at a café.

The questions could range from: How are you and what have you been doing the last few days? How has your day been, so far? How was your journey to the SSB? How do you like the environment at the SSB, the food and facilities at the candidates' mess and other such questions. He may also ask you to describe your journey or your hometown or place of residence. Once he is sure that you are comfortable, he will give you certain rules for the interview and then commence with the first round of questions.

The 40-odd minutes, thereafter, will go by in a flash, and you would have bared yourself to him in that time. During this time, he judges you to see if you can fit well to meet the armed forces' requirements. Just like the GTO and the Psychologist, he has his own way to check you out for the same qualities—the qualities that make a good officer.

The STAR method of answering questions:
When any question is asked, the best way to answer is the **STAR** method, where:
    S stands for Situation
    T for Tasks you were to do
    A for Action(s) taken
    R for Result of your action

Take the same example of the question posed to you about why your performance deteriorated in your final Board exam. The situation is about your performance deterioration, the task is that you needed to study hard, and the action you took was to not give adequate time to the studies due to xyz reason, and the result, obviously will be that you did not get the marks that you deserved.

Try the STAR method with other questions and you will see that you are able to give a correct, concise, and crisp answer. This method can be practised till it becomes second nature to you.

Towards the end of the interview, the interviewer will again indulge in small talk and ask you certain general questions. He will also ask you how your stay has been so far and if you have any questions or suggestions.

Generally, one cannot suddenly think of a question to ask, but if you have something which is out of the ordinary, go ahead and ask. Do not ask a question for the sake of asking or for impressing him, and certainly, do not ask him personal questions or ask him how you did in the interview; nor should you ask for any advice. After all, it is a test and he is there to evaluate you and you will soon know your result, anyway. As he ends, he will wish you luck and ask you to leave his office with your certificates.

Here are some interview essentials as an aid to your memory. They are self-explanatory and in bullet form:

Before the interview
- Practice responses to questions that may be asked. Do not learn your responses by heart.
- Body language is a very important part of communication.
- Mock interview-practice with your teacher, professor or friends is recommended.
- Rehearse your opening lines/pitch/volume.
- Rehearse your smile.
- Plan questions that you would like to ask (these are not necessary, and only if you must)
- Have a good, restful sleep and avoid caffeine.

Learn to relax
- Walk, run, meditate.
- Listen to music. It helps to calm your nerves.
- Practise positive self-talk. Talk in terms of I can, I will, I must!
- Think of positive outcomes.
- Be excited and not nervous.
- Remember—better preparation equals better confidence.

During the Interview
- Do not pretend.
- If you are nervous initially, you will not be faulted.
- Your honesty will be respected.
- Settle down fast (Remember to relax, relax…).
- Be yourself, and do not fake.
- Ask for a question to be repeated, only if not clear, not to buy time.
- Breathe normally, stay engaged and focused.
- Smile to ease tensions, and answer with a relevant anecdote if possible.
- Do not show you are desperate.
- Enjoy the process and tell yourself that it has a lot of learning value.

Golden tips for success
Some of these tips may be repetitive, but nevertheless, these are useful.
- 45 minutes to an hour is the 'make or break' time, so make the best use of this time.
- Start early, reach early, familiarise yourself with the surroundings, and make a mental note of the area.
- Know yourself: Introspection, SWOT Analysis.
- Read through your Self-Description, PIQ and PIQ tree.
- Maintain a positive attitude. Develop self-confidence. Do not take the interview lightly; don't be overconfident, either.
- Do not lie. That is a strict 'No'.
- Work on your communication skills. Be simple, clear, and use concise language.
- No dilly-dallying while answering questions; get straight to the point.

- Read newspapers and books. Good general awareness is a plus.
- Know details of the hobbies that you have.
- Revise your subjects. Your basics must be good and you should know your text books of the last three years.
- Give balanced answers based on facts. Your answers should be impartial, and show no social or political bias.
- Be prepared with justifications and examples from your life.
- Know your district and state well.
- Remain calm and collected. And if you don't know the answer, admit it.
- Maintain moral integrity and display high moral values.
- Use the internet for knowledge, not for generating controversy.
- Your body language should be sound. Remember the 80/20 rule and the 7-second rule.
- Speak to others who have gone through similar processes not during the SSB but during your preparations at home, so that you know what to expect.
- Avoid listening to rumours (and a lot of them are rampant on the internet).
- Drive the discussion.
- Follow a conservative dress code. In other words, carry whatever you wear elegantly. This builds your confidence.
- Check and recheck your documents and put them neatly in folders for easy accessibility.
- No watch, mobile or any gadget is permitted inside the interview room.

★ ★ ★

The Final Board Interview or Conference

> Success is not final; failure is not fatal; it is the courage
> to continue that counts.
> **–Winston Churchill**

By the fifth day, you are almost done with your SSB procedure. What remains is the final board interview or conference as it is called, held just before your departure. At some boards, GTO and interviews are planned for a few remaining candidates during the morning hours, while the final board interview is generally planned during the latter half of the day. The duty officer will brief you on the procedure and on your schedule.

He will tell you that you must appear for the interview in formal attire and that your bags must be packed and kept outside your rooms since you won't be allowed to go to your rooms after the final board interview. He will tell you that you will be made to sit at a convenient place near the Board-Conference room till you are called in order of your chest numbers.

The final board interview takes just a minute or two and it is here that your results of all the three rounds of tests are calculated and your fate decided by the assessors.

You will be seeing your assessors in uniform for the first

time and you may not even recognise them as they sit at a U-shaped table awaiting your arrival into the room. The board president sits at the head of the U while you are made to sit opposite him, in a chair placed in such a manner that all the assessors can look at you.

You may tend to be intimidated by the presence of so many uniformed officers, so take a few deep breaths before you enter. Before your entry, your performance would have been discussed and a decision taken whether you are good to go or not, based on the total marks that you have scored over the five days. If a candidate is a borderline case, he is discussed in detail and some additional questions may be posed to him by one of the members of the board.

In all cases, one of the members will ask candidates a few questions before they are asked to leave. The questions are basic, and since you will be more confident by now, you will give it your best shot. The result will be compiled after all the final board interviews are over, and soon you will be waiting in the auditorium to hear who is in and who is not—surely with butterflies in your stomach.

The president or his deputy will soon deliver the closing address after which the duty officer will announce the results. This is one tension-filled moment and the excitement and apprehension is palpable.

After the results are announced, successful candidates leave the hall to segregate their luggage since they will stay back for additional formalities.

The ones who didn't make it will be asked to gather for their departure formalities. They will receive their travel expenses and collect their mobiles. After this is done, they are escorted to the waiting buses which take them to the nearest railway or bus station for their return journeys.

Successful candidates need to fill up a lot more forms which may take another two hours and may have to stay an additional night at the Board. After this is done, they are routed to the nearest Military Hospital (MH) for their medical examination which could take three to four days. For Air Force aspirants, this medical exam is more stringent and is carried out at special units called the Air Force Central Medical Establishment or AFCME located at Delhi, Bangalore and Guwahati. The dates for the medical exam allotted to you may not be immediately after the SSB. In that case, you will be sent home and will have to report later directly to the MH or AFCME.

For IAF pilot aspirants, another series of tests are needed to be conducted. These were earlier called the Pilot Aptitude Battery Test (PABT) and were recently renamed as the Centralised Pilot Selection System (CPSS) test. These tests are done on the sixth day, only for the successful candidates.

This ends the hectic five-day schedule at the SSB—days that will remain etched in your mind for the rest of your life whether you made it or not and where you would have learnt some important life lessons, that will no doubt make you a better human being as well as also help you navigate through the difficulties of life.

For those of you who have made it through the SSB, this is the first tiny step forward in your resolve to join the armed forces. All that is left now is a rigorous medical exam as you await the final merit list to join the training academy of your choice. Once there, you will be transformed from boys and girls into young people of substance with a military bearing as first-class gazetted officers of the Indian Armed Forces!

The Final Board Interview or Conference | 137

Celebrate your success; you are now among that small elite percentage of people who have passed the most gruelling of job interviews in the country, perhaps.

For those who did not make it or for those who do not make it in the merit, there are many chances to reappear. Please do not give up. Failure should push you to work harder at your preparations for the SSB. I have known of candidates who have worked relentlessly and finally got through their SSB in their 16th attempt and more! So do not be disheartened, think positively, and get on with your academic life while continuing your efforts to join the armed forces.

Some candidates may not just be fit enough to join the armed forces for reasons best known to the assessors and certainly, they would have no reason to reject a deserving candidate. Know that any 'pull' or call from a politician or from 'above' can't help you pass.

You will hear negative and loose talk only from failed candidates. It is nothing but a reflection of mental weakness and such candidates want to blame everything else but themselves for their failure. Perhaps, that is the reason for their failure at the SSB. As I said earlier, at the SSB, you arrive with 100 per cent marks. As you go through the tests, your performance produces the negative marks that could lead to your failure!

I am sure you would have heard that great celebrities like our ex-President, Dr Abdul Kalam and superstar actor Amitabh Bachchan also appeared for the SSB and were rejected. They went on to become great men in other fields which shows the strength of their character! It also shows that when one door is closed for you, many others are still open!

If you get rejected at any stage in the testing process, don't take it to heart. Instead, choose one of the thousands of other avenues open today to you and become stalwarts in those fields or professions. But whatever you end up doing, your SSB experience will always come in handy wherever you are and wherever you go.

Body Language

People need realness, reality. People can sense when someone is pretentious or fake. It's because you feel it; it is in someone's body language.
–Afrojack

There are basically two means by which humans communicate with each other. The first is spoken or verbal language and the other is, non-verbal. We are aware of what spoken language skills are and why are they important from the SSB's point of view. I want to talk here about body language, part of non-verbal communication skills.

Non-verbal communication deals with our gestures or gesticulations, facial expressions, posture, and eye contact, all of which are used along with our verbal expression. The assessors at the SSB are taught about body language and are well-versed to judge your over-all personality.

In this short chapter, I will not go into details of the subject, but want to acquaint you with the basics, just so that you put your best foot forward while at the SSB, and in life, as well.

Only 7 per cent of our communication is verbal; the rest is non-verbal which means we convey more through non-verbal communication than otherwise! Of the 93 per cent non-verbal communication, our tone, pitch, pauses, and vocal stress on words convey 38 per cent of what we mean while the rest 55 per cent is taken up by pure non-verbal communication, termed as 'Body Language.'

We will discuss some key points of body language over the next few pages.

Facial expression

When you look at someone, your face gives away the way you feel about the person. You may look at him or her lovingly, your eyebrows may be up to express surprise, while your smile reveals if you are genuinely happy or not. Your cheeks can reveal your level of excitement or confidence and more. Frothing at your mouth or excess salivation are signs of nervousness. You might have experienced all these emotions, yourself, but perhaps, would not have put two and two together.

Eye contact

Eye contact is very important in non-verbal communication. When you maintain eye contact when someone is speaking to you or when you are speaking with someone, it will show that you are confident and attentive. You must have gone through situations when your mother or teacher has been angry with you and has conveyed the same by glaring at you. The pupils of the eye dilate or constrict depending on your mood and this can be easily seen by the person you are conversing with.

Sometimes, if you stare at someone, you end up making that person uncomfortable and communication becomes difficult. You must have experienced this. Eyes can show respect and disrespect, show if you are attentive and polite and convey if you are a shy or introverted.

In my personal experience in interviewing, I have found

that eyes reveal the real you in more ways than one, and I have always made a note of how the candidates maintains eye contact when they speak with me. I could also make out when a candidate was not speaking the truth or speaking something that he did not mean. His eyes would flinch! Eyes are the most difficult to mask, and if you can do it, perhaps, you should join the theatre!

There are some candidates, too, who I found talking to the ceiling as they refused to look at me in the eye!

Hand gestures/body movements

You would have seen that a lot of people gesticulate with their hands while they speak. Purposeful hand movements can emphasise points, convey enthusiasm, or add clarity to a verbal message. At the same time, if hand movements are overdone, it distracts the person you are speaking with and may cause irritation, eventually leading to breakdown of communication. When one is asked to speak at a formal function, one needs to keep gesticulation to the minimum, you will agree.

At the SSB too, the best would be to keep your hand gestures to a minimum since most of the solo talks including the interview are semi-formal. Even if you keep moving your hands to your face or run them through your hair, or play with your fingers, shake your legs while speaking or are fidgety when you sit, it conveys that you lack confidence and are nervous.

Posture

How we walk, stand, and carry ourselves also talks about our personality. I have seen many boys and girls come for the interview and sit in a most unnatural manner as they are taught in some of the training centres. They stretch their arms and sit with their palms facing downwards on their knees in a stiff manner. Not only does this take away their energy while maintaining this pose, it also keeps them uncomfortable during the interview.

On the other hand, what would you think of a person who slouches and walks with his head down? Whether it is sitting or standing, our posture conveys confidence, openness, or discomfort.

Handshakes

Some interviewers or the GTO may shake hands with you. A strong handshake can leave a lasting impression and signifies trust, respect, and professionalism. I have noticed some candidates giving an extremely firm, almost knuckle-grinding and painful handshake, which is best avoided. Similarly, a weak handshake also has its own misgivings.

Remember, our bodies speak volumes even when we are silent. Pay attention to your own body language and observe others. This is a fascinating aspect of human interactions!

It will be good to know a few more aspects about body language, even though they may not be really applicable to the SSB process. These are about 'touch' and 'space.'

Touch

We communicate a great deal through touch. A tap on the shoulder, a reassuring squeeze of the arm, a hug or a pat on the head do mean a great deal, don't they? You may see this kind of communication taking place between candidates when you do your GTO tests. But besides a formal handshake at the interview, you are not likely to experience this kind of communication with officials at the SSB.

Space

The other aspect of communication is about 'space.' Have you ever felt uncomfortable when someone stands too close to you and speaks, almost intruding into your space? All of us have a need for physical space and this need depends on the relationship, situation, and the culture that you come from. The closer you are to someone in any relationship, the closer you will allow him or her to come closer, physically. When you meet your SSB mates on the first day, you will maintain a distance when you interact, but as the days go by, and especially at the end of group tasks, I have observed candidates hugging each other, holding hands and being more physical; sometimes, it looks as if they have been close friends for years!

Physical space is used to communicate signals of intimacy, aggression, dominance, or affection.

Tone and tenor

It is important for you to understand that the tone, pitch, volume, inflection, rhythm, and rate at which you speak are also significant non-verbal communicators. When we speak, other people 'read' our voice in addition to listening to our words. These non-verbal sounds provide subtle but powerful clues to our true feelings and what we really mean. For example, think of how your tone can indicate sarcasm, anger, affection, or even confidence.

Impact of body language on communication

Body language significantly impacts communication in various contexts, including in personal relationships, professional settings, and public speaking.

Personal relationships

Body language plays a vital role in expressing emotions and building connections. Positive body language, such as maintaining eye contact, nodding, and open gestures, fosters trust and rapport. Conversely, negative body language such as crossed arms, lack of eye contact, and fidgeting, can create barriers and lead to misunderstandings.

Professional settings

In professional settings, effective use of body language can enhance leadership, teamwork, and negotiation skills. Leaders who exhibit confident body language inspire trust and respect from their team members. During negotiations, reading the body language of others can provide valuable insights into their level of interest, agreement, or resistance.

Public speaking

Public speakers rely on body language to engage their audience and reinforce their message. Gestures, facial expressions, and eye contact help to emphasise points, convey enthusiasm, and maintain audience interest. Effective body language can make a speech more compelling and memorable.

Conclusion

Body language is a powerful form of communication that transcends words. Its components—gestures, facial expressions, posture, eye movements, and proxemics—each contribute to the overall message being conveyed. Understanding and effectively utilising body language can enhance personal relationships, professional interactions, and public speaking abilities. As a universal language, body language has the potential to bridge cultural divides and foster better understanding among people. Recognising its significance and learning to interpret nonverbal cues can lead to more effective and meaningful communication.

The PABT or CPSS - The Pilot Aptitude Test for IAF Pilot Entry

Once you have tasted flight, you will forever walk the earth with your eyes turned skyward, for there you have been, and there you will always long to return.
–Leonardo da Vinci

In earlier times, the test that we underwent for pilot entry into the Air Force (and aviation branches of the Army and the Navy) was called the Pilot Aptitude Battery Test or the PABT. Now, in the age of computers, a bigger and better test has made its way into the SSB called the Computerised Pilot Selection System or the CPSS. This computer-based module has been specially designed to check aspirants for their aptitude in trainability for flying technologically advanced machines.

This system has been designed and developed by our Defence Research Development Organisation (DRDO) and is operational at the SSBs in Dehradun, Varanasi, and Mysore.

This is a once-in-a-lifetime test; and if you fail this, you cannot become a military pilot in any of the three services as well as in the Coast Guard. However, there is no embargo or rule which says that a candidate who has failed this test cannot become a civil aviation pilot.

The test is conducted in two parts.

The Cognitive Ability Test

The first part is called the INS-B test or the cognitive ability test and is a test of your mental faculty. It is designed to test your mental capacity and capability to solve simple problems in your mind. The test is administered in two parts.

In the first part, you shall have to answer some basic mathematics questions as well as questions related to reasoning ability, mental geometry, and visualisation. In the second part, you will answer some simple questions related to aircraft instrument indications.

For this second part of the test, you will get a detailed briefing by one of the pilots posted at the SSB. Some of the basic instruments of an aircraft and their indications or readings will be explained to you in detail along with examples. After all your doubts are cleared, you will attempt this part of the test.

The Cognitive Testing Hall

The Psychomotor Test

The Psychomotor Test is conducted in a cockpit-like environment as shown in the photograph here. The cockpit has a computer screen on which you will have to play 10 'games' for which you will be briefed thoroughly. You will also get to practice the games once and then appear for the test once you are ready.

In this aircraft simulator-like-cockpit, the candidate is required to operate the aircraft controls like control stick, rudder, throttle and attend to various aural and visual warning systems. The visual system will require you to operate a switch whenever a warning light illuminates while the audio warning will have to be put off by operating another switch whilst you are continuing with the test (in reality, a computer game). This is to see if your brain can multitask under stress. This test also checks your hand-to-eye coordination and motor functions that are required to operate technologically advanced aircraft.

The test is simple. If you have played video games, then you should be able to score the required marks without a problem. I have seen that most of the candidates now pass this test with ease.

You really do not have to prepare for this test at all. Some of the training institutes have tried to copy this test to familiarise candidates, but their systems are nowhere close to the one employed by the SSB.

As always, be relaxed and have your wits about you and you should be able to pass this test with ease! You could do further research on the internet, but if you ask me, I do not think that necessary.

The Psychomotor Test Hall

Once this test is complete, the selected candidates are sent for medicals after which they return home awaiting their merit list and call letters. For those who do not pass this test, you are allowed to opt for the other two services or you can opt for ground duty branches of the IAF.

Epilogue

> If you want a happy onding, that depends, of course, on where you stop your story!
> –Orson Welles

Well then, that's it. This is what the SSB is all about. Come to think of it, it is quite simple really!

When I went for my selection to the Air Force Selection Board (AFSB), many years ago, I was not yet sixteen! Having led a very sheltered and simple life till then, I was shy, naïve, raw and a little stressed and underconfident. Although I had not gone through any formal training for the SSB, I was lucky that I had received good schooling and parenting in my formative years. I do believe that this, along with my innate curiosity and inquisitive nature helped me to get through the process in my first attempt.

As I became the president of the same SSB that passed me many years later, I was lucky to understand the scientific nature of the system that had selected me. The doubts and misconceptions about the process that I had carried through my service career were now laid to rest. I understood that the system was robust, having stood the test of time, and I understood that with the processes executed correctly, we were sure of selecting the right candidates as leaders for one of the largest armed forces in the world.

Over the years, the SSB procedure has been analysed down to its bare nuts and bolts by many assessors and self-proclaimed experts who have written fat volumes on the subject. The internet is also full of information on the SSB and many sites are money-spinners, earning from the candidates who register with them.

My endeavour here has been to demystify the whole process and tell you that it is best to prepare for each of the tests yourself, rather than spend thousands of rupees to learn some shortcuts to success, which may not always work.

The assessors at the SSB, too, are happiest when they test fresh and untrained candidates, rather than the 'smart alec,' coached ones. This is not because of any bias, but because a raw candidate is always open, natural, and often comes up with some good new ideas during the planning and plotting that happens during the tests. I was always thrilled to grill such a candidate in my interviews because I received replies that were unique and new—and there was something that I, too, could learn from them. My colleagues, the GTOs and Psychologists will also agree with me wholeheartedly, I am sure.

It, by no means implies that assessors are against trained candidates. If they have imbibed the correct things during their exposure to training, it serves them well; otherwise, most candidates appear to be doing a cut-paste and copy job. And when this happens, it can get a trifle irritating for the assessors who must then dig deeper to find out about the **real** you. So, by all means go for training academies, but choose wisely the academy that trains correctly. Treat the success rates they proclaim with caution. Remember that statistics can be twisted to lure candidates!

All through this book I have asked you the following for good chances of success. At the cost of repetition, here they are, once more:

(a) Prepare well. Be aware of your surroundings and of what is happening around you as well as know your armed forces.//
(b) Practice the art of reading, writing, and speaking in English.//
(c) Know yourself, be yourself, and have faith in yourself.//
(d) Keep calm and be alert so that you think logically even under duress.//
(e) Learn to deal with mental stress; know the symptoms and the ways to deal with it. **Do not give up at any stage.**//
(f) Last, but not the least, become a good human being! That is most important!

★ ★ ★

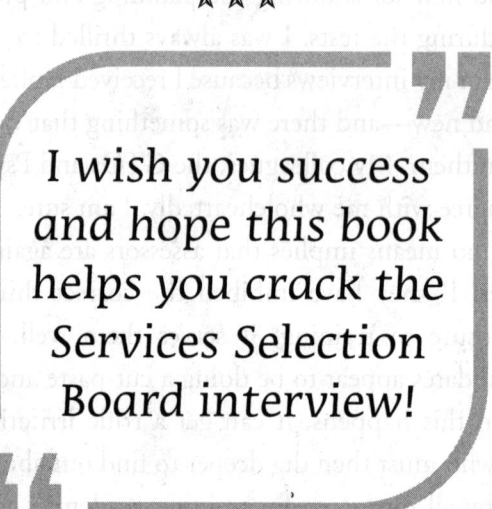

> I wish you success and hope this book helps you crack the Services Selection Board interview!

Should you have any questions, you can connect with me at nitinsathe. talks@ssb.com or through my website, nitinsathe.com